DRIVING SUSTAINABILITY TO BUSINESS SUCCESS

DRIVING SUSTAINABILITY TO BUSINESS SUCCESS

The DS Factor–Management System Integration and Automation

M. Jayne Pilot,
EP(CEA), EP(EMSLA), CPEA, CEO,
Pilot Performance Resources
Management Inc.

WILEY

Cover Design: Wiley
Cover Image: © iStock.com / arcady_31

Published by John Wiley & Sons, Inc., Hoboken, New Jersey.
Published simultaneously in Canada.

For general information on our other products and services or for technical support, please contact our Customer Care Department within the United States at (800) 762-2974, outside the United States at (317) 572-3993 or fax (317) 572-4002.

Wiley publishes in a variety of print and electronic formats and by print-on-demand. Some material included with standard print versions of this book may not be included in e-books or in print-on-demand. If this book refers to media such as a CD or DVD that is not included in the version you purchased, you may download this material at http://booksupport.wiley.com. For more information about Wiley products, visit www.wiley.com.

Library of Congress Cataloging-in-Publication Data:

Pilot, M. Jayne.
   Driving sustainability to business success: management system integration and automation—the DS factor/Jayne Pilot.
      pages cm. — (Wiley corporate F&A series)
   Includes index.
   ISBN 978-1-118-35693-7 (hardback); ISBN 978-1-118-42026-3 (ebk); ISBN 978-1-118-41693-8 (ebk)   1. Organizational effectiveness.   2. Management.   I. Title.
   HD58.9.P55 2014
   658.4′08—dc23

                                                              2014023473

Printed in the United States of America

10 9 8 7 6 5 4 3 2 1

Contents

Preface

Sustainability is of the utmost importance in the minds of CEOs in today's world. This book outlines some of the organizations and leaders driving this initiative, with the differences in what the term *sustainability* means. Not just an environmentally sustainable design, but a business pathway with the ability to sustain success.

Leaders have many challenges facing them in the coming years, as they set the strategy, vision, culture, and leadership of the management team for their companies or organizations.

The grey tsunami is one challenge, where the baby boomers are leaving the workforce, replaced by the new manager, who understands technological innovation but maybe does not understand past business performance of the organization to bring about organizational innovation.

It is the foundation that will be laid now by the new CEOs or leaders that will make a difference in our world by creating new value-added products, processes, and business models through innovation for sustainability for the future.

Great leaders are those people who ask thought-provoking questions, who may not always have the right answers, but have the ability to have the courage to ask, analyze information, make decisions, and bring about change to drive the success of the business.

Working with many organizations helped me to see the pitfalls in process operations and management system structures. I realized that the success of the company started first with management's principles and then the management system structure. Companies have implemented many management systems separately but could save time and money by integrating and automating management systems, preventing duplication in documentation and activities, and streamlining analysis of data.

This book was written to provide insight and inspiration for leaders, CEOs, managers, and service providers to assist them in being a driving force behind sustainability for businesses. With this in mind, the book addresses business principles and management system structure with the need to address risks.

It provides an opportunity for the reader to Assess, Reflect, and Act, in order to drive business success. Space is provided in the book for you to apply the concepts of principles to your own business and answer questions to stimulate action to bring people, process, and technology together for business success. It is your leadership planning that drives the changes that will bring growth, structure, and expansion to your business.

Audience

The readers of this book on "Driving Business Sustainability" are senior managers, presidents, CEOs, CFOs, owners, entrepreneurs, accountants, consultants, and students wishing to be leaders in business management. This book is intended as a resource that will assist them to review the business principles and management system structure that will build a strong framework to drive business success.

Overview of the Contents

Sustainability has many definitions. In Part I of the book, the term sustainability is examined as used by the United Nations, Dow Jones, and Pilot Performance Resources Management Inc.

The UN Global Compact—Accenture CEO Study on Sustainability had more than 1,000 top executives, from 27 industries across 103 countries, review sustainability. CEOs see that the barrier to embedding the UN thinking on sustainability into the organization is a lack of a link between sustainability and business value. This is an opportunity for you to view some of their findings and principles for sustainability with lessons from the leaders.

There are many organizations bringing change and improvements in our world to be sustainable. The book references the inspirational video *Children of the Dump Project* and the "Moringa Tree" project, and how innovation makes a change with the motto, "Helping People Help People."

Corporate responsibility to sustainability has been directed and supported by the International Institute for Sustainable Development, and many organizations use the Global Reporting Initiative's (GRI) "Sustainability Reporting Framework." The KPMG survey on "Corporate Responsibility Reporting" outlines the lessons from the leaders, one being to establish robust systems and processes.

My definition of sustainability is directed to business and its "ability" to "sustain," to drive its organization now into the future.

Part II addresses international principles, codes of conduct, and essential characteristics for effective and efficient operation of an organization. Principles provide leaders with the five Ps: Possibilities, Priorities, Performance, Productivity, and Profits. This part of the book gives you as a leader an opportunity to document questions applicable to your own business to use as reference.

Part III, connecting with the global business world, looks to international management systems that business leaders utilize and the need for integration and standardization of these management systems. I present my "Three-Step Process—Identify, Insure, Improve"™ for management system implementation and the management of risks. The focus in this part is on key questions for you to answer that will inspire and direct you in the changes to make for your success.

You are the leader to drive business sustainability in this competitive landscape. Planned change through the "Management System Makeover"™ is outlined in the book for you to assess, reflect, and act.

Acknowledgments

Writing a book of this nature is a challenge. I would like to thank Google's innovators, Larry Page and Sergey Brin, for their mission in 1996 to organize the world's information and make it universally accessible and useful. This gave me the ability to research at the click of a key to find data and information. Google understands driving business sustainability and is innovative, believing in acquisitions and partnerships.

The leaders of sustainability are all of you who takes on the challenge and bring about a change to improve the world in which we live.

Thank you to all the many companies I have worked with throughout my business life, from registrars, standards bodies, and government to industry, institutions, and many nonprofit organizations and committees, who have provided me with insight about how organizations function and how leaders think and operate. I cannot name them as there are too many and it is difficult to choose which to leave out.

Asking questions is not unfamiliar to me; my mother joked that the reason I always ask "why" is because she named me Jayne with a y. The business leaders of today who ask questions are taking the first step to sustainability.

I would like to personally thank Sharon Wilson, my dear friend and a high school English teacher, for her support and review of my book.

In addition, I am honored to have had the opportunity to work with John Wiley & Sons and bring this information to the global marketplace.

PART I

Business Sustainability

T he United Nations outlined on its website that "sustainability calls for a decent standard of living for everyone today without compromising the needs of future generations."

We are all partners in maintaining sustainability of our world's quality, environment, health, and safety management, impacting billions of people around the world. Global adversity trends include: food scarcity, depletion of natural resources, major climate change, water quality, extinction of animals, quality control on products, and globalization—carrying out business around the world.

The role of companies has been changing, especially in developing countries, where it is crucial for businesses that enter into these marketplaces to go beyond their core business lines and help to improve education, protect the environment, and address poverty and human rights, and, as a result, enhance their reputations and business models.

Many industries have been criticized for their lack of sustainability practices for some time now. In response, governments are implementing new legislation and regulations to provide accelerated changes in areas related to climate change, energy conservation, and the health and safety of workers.

Companies at first viewed the "green" movement as a threat. Today "going green" helps companies stay out of the "red" with actions taken to reduce consumption of energy and alternate methods for energy and management of resources. This is what I call the green sustainability movement. Companies are showing the world that they are credible sustainers of our world. Al Gore's documentary, *An Inconvenient Truth*, moved many CEOs and has been credited with raising international public awareness of climate change and the environmental movement.

The TED Talks daily video podcast on YouTube is another resource that has impacted millions around the world. A young girl, Maya Penn, was featured on TED Talks (February 2014). She started her first company when she was eight years old. Many CEOs can learn a lot from this young entrepreneur, who values not only creativity and innovation but also her responsibility to the planet.

There are many definitions of sustainability. From reports outlined on sustainability, many companies are evaluating what this term means to them. Part I in this book, focuses on the terms for sustainability and the focus of top business leaders in this area. For sustainability to assist an organization it needs to provide value to the company; that is why I look at the definition of sustainability first, then in Part II, I move to the principles that can make a business successful with the support of an integrated management system that meets international standards in order to operate in the global marketplace, as described in Part III.

CHAPTER 1

CEO Study on Sustainability

A n excellent report called "The UN Global Compact-Accenture CEO Study on Sustainability 2013, Architects of a Better World" is one of the world's largest CEO studies on sustainability to date. It had more than 1,000 top executives from 27 industries across 103 countries discuss a new global architecture for businesses contributing to global priorities.

Peter Lacy, CEO Study Lead and Managing Director of Accenture Strategy & Sustainability Asia Pacific, outlined in the introduction that sustainability has become established on the leadership agenda of almost every leading business.

He wrote that "This year is a unique opportunity to take stock as we stand at a crossroads in the global economy. Business leaders are committed to leading the way, but will require greater ambition and wider support as they work to align sustainability impact with value creation, and markets with sustainable development outcomes, such that business leaders can truly become the architects of a better world."[1]

Refocus of Business Leaders—Top Priorities

Business leaders are refocusing, and the report shows that two thirds of responding CEOs outlined the following top three priorities for the future success of their business:

1. Growth and employment: 64 percent
2. Education: 40 percent
3. Energy: 39 percent

Link between Sustainability and Business Value

CEOs were asked as part of the study, what barriers they had to further progress in embedding sustainability into their organization. CEOs saw one factor arising more than any other over the past decade: the **lack of a link between sustainability and business value**. CEOs are clear that action must be justified against traditional **measures of success**.[1]

The report lists two areas for the agenda for action:

1. Government intervention to align public policy with sustainability at global, national, and local levels, including hard measures on regulations, standards, and taxation
2. Company sharing, to learn from others who are already leading the way, harnessing sustainability as an opportunity for innovation and growth, and delivering business value and sustainability impact at scale

United Nations Global Compact: The Ten Principles— Understanding Their Scope of Sustainability

Throughout the report, the term *sustainability* encompasses environmental, social, and corporate governance. The ten principles the United Nations Global Compact asks companies to embrace, support, and enact within their sphere of influence are as follows:

Human Rights

Principle 1:   Businesses should support and respect the internationally proclaimed human rights.

Principle 2:   Make sure that they are not complicit in human rights abuses.

Labour

Principle 3:   Businesses should uphold the freedom of association and the effective recognition of the right to collective bargaining.

Principle 4:   The elimination of all forms of forced and compulsory labor.

Principle 5:   The effective abolition of child labour.

Principle 6:   The elimination of discrimination in respect of employment and occupation.

Environment

Principle 7:   Businesses should support a precautionary approach to environmental challenges.

Principle 8:   Undertake initiatives to promote greater environmental responsibility.

Principle 9:   Encourage the development and diffusion of environmentally friendly technologies.

Anti-Corruption

Principle 10:   Businesses should work against corruption in all its forms, including extortion and bribery.

Seven Steps to Sustainability

From the research and analysis done, the report outlined, as follows, that leaders are approaching sustainability differently. CEOs see seven key themes that guide their thinking and actions, which transform strategies, business models, value chains, and industries in order to achieve leadership in sustainability and high performance.

Step 1: Realism and context—understanding the scale of the challenge and the opportunity.

Step 2: Growth and differentiation—turning sustainability to advantage and value creation.

Step 3: Value and performance—"what gets measured gets managed;" quantifying the value of sustainability initiatives, more sustainable business models, track impact on communities.

Step 4: Technology and innovation—new models for success; investment in renewables, intelligent infrastructure enabled by machine-to-machine communication, closed-loop business models, innovative R&D, cloud computing, analytics, etc.

Step 5: Partnerships and collaboration—new challenges, new solutions; close partnerships with governments, policymakers, industry peers, consumers, and NGOs.

Step 6: Engagement and dialogue—broadening the conversation; two-way dialogue—engaging stakeholders (consumers and local communities, regulators and policy makers, investors and shareholders, employees and labor unions) to negotiate role of business in addressing global challenges.

Step 7: Advocacy and leadership—shaping future systems; collaborative solutions with governments and other stakeholders; business leaders' advocacy and public commitment is integral to progress.

Will the pace of change address the global challenges to be able to support a population of nine billion by 2050? Time will tell.

CEOs on Sustainability

The report shows that business leaders are successful in making the case for sustainability within their organizations.

- Eighty-four percent of CEOs report that it is discussed and acted on at the board level.
- Seventy-eight percent of CEOs see sustainability as an opportunity for growth and innovation.
- Eighty percent see it as a route to competitive advantage in the industry.

TABLE 1.1		
CEOs' Perception of the Importance of Sustainability Varies by Industry		
Industry*	Important	Very Important
Utilities	39%	61%
Banking	39	61
Infrastructure & Transportation Services	50	48
Chemicals	47	50
Metals & Mining	43	54
Communications	63	33
Automotive	52	43
Consumer Goods & Services	41	53
Energy	35	59
Industrial Equipment	54	38
Electronics and High Tech	46	42

*Based on 1,000 completed responses.

Source: UNGC-Accenture CEO Study 2013.

The importance of sustainability can vary from industry to industry; see Table 1.1

Siemens is one company outlined in the report. It has achieved strong growth throughout the downturn through a focus on innovative technologies in clean energy (offshore wind turbines), enabling customers to cut CO_2 emissions worldwide and develop intelligent infrastructure.

CEO Learnings[2]

You will not be judged anymore only by the top line or bottom line results in your company. You will increasingly be judged by the contributions that you will make to society.

Paul Polman, Unilever

The world is more complex, and risks are more interconnected; but a complex world is an opportunity, if you can deal with its complexity.

Martin Senn, Zurich Insurance Group

We measure our success not by the profit we make, but by the difference we make.

Bob Collymore, Safaricom Ltd.

The role of every company is to be a positive force in society: you have to focus on creating value, creating success, and if you look from the perspective of the long term then in going about your business you should engage with society positively.

Carlos Brito, Anheuser-Busch InBev

There is a natural evolution in the investment community towards sustainability, corporate governance and transparency: these will soon become normal parts of the investor discussion.

Federico Ghizzoni, UniCredit

To accelerate progress on sustainability, we need governments to recognize the role of business as a solution in providing growth and innovation.

Sir Andrew Witty, GlaxoSmithKline

Assess & Reflect #1

HOW IMPORTANT ARE SUSTAINABILITY ISSUES TO THE FUTURE SUCCESS OF YOUR BUSINESS?

_____
_____
_____
_____
_____
_____
_____
_____
_____
_____
_____
_____
_____
_____
_____
_____
_____
_____
_____
_____
_____
_____
_____
_____
_____
_____
_____
_____
_____
_____
_____
_____
_____
_____

Assess & Reflect #2

WHAT WOULD OUR COMPANY'S QUOTE BE ON BUSINESS SUSTAINABILITY?

_____
_____
_____
_____
_____
_____
_____
_____
_____
_____
_____
_____
_____
_____
_____
_____
_____
_____
_____
_____
_____
_____
_____
_____
_____
_____
_____
_____
_____
_____
_____
_____
_____
_____
_____
_____
_____

Quantify Business Value for Sustainability

The UN Global Compact-Accenture CEO Study on Sustainability states that sustainability must lead to business value. Sometimes the rewards tied with sustainability are hard to quantify. While they may reduce risk, sometimes the benefits are not seen right away, especially if they have not been measured.

The report states that only 57 percent of CEOs could set out in detail their strategies for seizing the opportunities presented by sustainability over the next five years. It is also startling to learn that only 38 percent were able to accurately quantify the business value of their companies' sustainability initiatives.

The question I would ask of the 1,000+ top executives is, **"What criteria are you managing your business to?"**

Measurement is one of the key seven steps outlined earlier to the UN's sustainability, under "Value and Performance." Measurement is crucial in improving the efficiency and effectiveness of any business.

Also, if companies have management system structures in place to international standards (ISO - International Organization for Standardization), which most of the large international companies do, then they are required to not only identify risks in their processes, but also establish, monitor, measure, and evaluate business objectives and targets (initiatives) throughout the organization to improve.

One flaw I see is that ISO's management systems do not outline or emphasize the need to tie management system processes, including objectives, to the financial bottom line and this is where the CEOs' and CFOs' focus is.

My years of auditing major corporations have shown me that many companies are working on many projects; however, they do not have systems in place for central tracking of what projects are being done, by whom, and when, and the costs associated with the organization's bottom line.

Companies need integrated management systems tied to financials in order to be in control of all departments; this tracks their controls and measurements for all processes for sustainability.

Another flaw I have seen is that the CEOs and CFOs have limited understanding of what the International Standards requirements are for their registered managements systems.

Factors Driving CEOs on Sustainability

The factors in order of priority that currently drive CEOs to take action on sustainability issues according to the report are as follows:

- Brand, trust, and reputation: 69 percent
- Potential for revenue growth/cost reduction: 49 percent
- Consumer/customer demand: 47 percent
- Personal motivation: 41 percent
- Employee engagement and recruitment: 38 percent
- Governmental/regulatory environment: 27 percent
- Impact of development gaps on business (e.g., water, food, poverty, infrastructure): 15 percent
- Pressure from investors/shareholders: 12 percent
- Other: 3 percent

It is interesting to note that investors are not a critical driver for companies to take action on sustainability. CEOs may need to communicate better with investors about how sustainability initiatives are aligned to their strategy, financial performance, and valuation. A study will be done in 2014 on investors and asset managers who represent nearly $35 trillion in assets and will be available at www.accenture.com/ungcstudy.

Another study will be done by Accenture and the Global Compact, partnering with Havas, to understand what drives consumer preferences and behaviors on sustainability, which will be available in 2014.[3]

Note

1. "UN Global Compact-Accenture CEO Study on Sustainability 2013 Report," www.accenture.com/us-en/sustainability/Pages /sustainability-index.aspx.
2. Ibid.
3. Ibid.

CHAPTER 2

Sustainability in Developing Countries— Innovation

DevXchange

Many service organizations work to help sustainability in our world, such as Rotary International (with over 1.2 members) and Rotary clubs (220 countries), as well as many other nonprofit organizations. Many leaders and managers are members of this organization, as I am, providing community service to improve quality of life in not only their communities but internationally. Microsoft India and Rotary International District 3010 in July 2014 signed a memorandum of understanding to provide Microsoft IT Academy Program in 150 Delhi NCR schools, covering over 150,000 students and 7,500 educators.[1] Another mission of Rotary is to eradicate polio worldwide.

DevXchange is a different type of organization that has made a difference in developing countries. This organization is one of volunteers, led by Bob Black, which prefers to work through "agents" or locally registered indigenous partners. This cuts down on its overhead costs, contributes to the sustainability of project interventions, and puts ownership and management of the project in the hands of those who best understand how to positively impact the lives of their own people.

Its mission is the following: "To help individuals and communities actualize just, peaceful and sustainable futures by facilitating innovative and effective interventions in developing countries, through a development exchange that contributes to the positive development of body, soul and spirit of both donor and recipient."[2]

Children of the Dump Project

A heartrending video called *Children of the Dump*, by Dave Parry, which can be viewed on his site at www.davemakesitmove.com/africa.html or YouTube, shows how a dump is a home for 8,000 people in the city of Addis Abba, Ethiopia. This situation exists not just in this country but in many.

The city houses around 10 million people, with about 1 million who live on the street. The poorest of the poor are the people who live on the dump: women, children, and the elderly. Their home is made out of whatever they can get from the dump, where often nine families share a makeshift room, with five or more people in a bed. Their existence goes from day to day, and many people are infected with leprosy and HIV.

DevXchange volunteers based out of Canada have assisted in Ethiopia to bring about sustainability, to make a change. A program called Bethal Fund was initiated by one of the people who survived living on the dump and is now leading the project to help other children of the dump by providing food, clothing, medical services, and a place to go to school. It gives the children an opportunity to get out of the dump. Please help the program through corporate donations to make a difference in a child's life (see Figure 2.1).

Helping People Help People

The vision of DevXchange to help the world for sustainability by helping people help people is making a difference. The planting of the Moringa tree brought about a radical change to the Gumuz tribe, helping

FIGURE 2.1

Children of the Dump

Dave Parry, Photographer (www.davemakesitmove.com/africa.html)

to reduce the spread of malaria and HIV/AIDS, improving their health and bringing about sustainability for them and their land.

The video *The Gumuz*, by Dave Parry, shows the importance of sustainability for this tribe in Western Ethiopia near the Nile River. The Gumuz are primitive, with a history of violence and intertribal fighting. This tribe takes what they need from the land, still hunting with bow and arrow and then leaving the land, which was once a lush jungle with vast forests of bamboo, barren. To survive they have killed off most of the wildlife and destroyed much of the environment, selling wood for charcoal.

The mortality rate for children under five is over 50 percent. Children are taught to kill when they are toddlers. People were afraid to go to help the tribe due to their violent nature. This tribe faced serious health challenges, such as malnutrition, malaria, and HIV/AIDS (see Figure 2.2).

FIGURE 2.2

Before: No Sustainability in This "Bush-Savanna" Region, a Barren Area

Dave Parry, photographer (www.davemakesitmove.com/Africa.html).

Moringa Tree Known as "Miracle Tree" for Sustainability

Innovation is key not only for business but also for organizations that work to bring an improved quality of life for the poor and hungry.

DevXchange had a vision and worked on a pilot project in Ethiopia for over three years, planting 300,000 Moringa trees, better known as

FIGURE 2.3

After: Gumuz Agro Forestry Program

Dave Parry, photographer (www.davemakesitmove.com/africa.html).

the miracle tree, and teaching better forest-management techniques and farming methods with soil-conservation practices.

The leaves of this fast-growing tree can be eaten and have been found to prevent and cure malaria. The foliage has three times more iron than spinach, as much protein as eggs, seven times more vitamin C than oranges, four times more vitamin A than carrots, four times more calcium than milk, and three times more potassium than bananas. In its first year the drought-tolerant Moringa can reach a height of three meters and grows best in arid conditions. (See Figure 2.3.)

Notes

1. For Rotary and Microsoft news, go to http://tech.firstpost.com /news-analysis/microsoft-india-rotary-international-district-partner-provide-technology-training-150-delhi-schools-226845.html.

2. For more information on DevXchange and the Gumuz Agro Forestry Program go to www.devxchange.org.

CHAPTER 3

Sustainability in the Banking Community

I n the banking sector, new standards and codes of conduct have been promoting corporate accountability, the need for transparency, and the need for management of risks for environment and society. They have recognized the need for sustainability as part of financing.

The traditional approach of the banking sector to sustainability needed to be adjusted, as financial statements alone did not present the whole picture of the sustainability of the business. Under this type of review, potential environmental liabilities, such as decommissioning costs that can create financial risks, can go undetected unless disclosed by the borrower. This may then impair the borrower in repaying the loan. Banks now look to new programs designed for environmental business.

International Finance Corporation—IFC Financing in Emerging Markets

IFC's definition of sustainability as outlined in its "Banking on Sustainability" report is about ensuring long-term business success while contributing toward economic and social development, a healthy environment, and a stable society.

Chris Coulter, vice president of GlobeScan Inc. (international public opinion researchers), from "Banking on Sustainability – Financing

Environmental and Social Opportunities in Emerging Markets" IFC, World Bank Group outlined is quoted in the report:

> The role of companies in a society is currently going through a transition that presents important opportunities and, in many ways, is being felt most strongly in developing economies.
>
> Expectations are highest in the developing world for the private sector to go beyond core business lines to help improve education and health systems, address poverty, protect the environment and reinforce human rights.
>
> By responding effectively to these expectations, local companies can not only protect and enhance their reputations, but also ensure that they are on equal footing with multinational corporations entering their markets.

IFC—which is the private-sector lending arm for the World Bank Group—looks to Environment, Social and Governance (ESG) criteria in its portfolio analysis of investments. Institutional investors are fully concerned with the extent to which management of quality and long-term returns is being controlled within companies.

Banks are increasingly moving from avoiding risks to creating sustainable banking opportunities, where sustainable development is seen as an advantage and opportunity for growth.

Due to information being accessible so quickly through the web, all organizations including the banks need to handle social and environmental risks. The report outlines that the majority of banks ranked the risks of negative publicity and loss of reputation (83 percent) as the number-one long-term risk, more important than credit risk—unwilling or unable to fulfill contractual obligations (68 percent) and security-devalued collateral (49 percent).

Banks' perceptions of key social and environmental risks facing their clients in order of priority were: disruption of operations, environmental legal issues, health and safety for workers, loss of market share because of environmental regulations, market devaluation because of social or environmental liability, loss of liability insurance coverage, and other.

Sustainable Finance Awards

The *Financial Times* and IFC launched the Annual FT/IFC Sustainable Finance Awards for financial institutions that show leadership and dedication in integrating environmental, social, and corporate governance into their business.

They have five categories: Sustainable Bank, Investor, Investment, Technology in Sustainable Finance, and Achievement in Inclusive Business.

In June 2013 in London the winners were announced, with M-KOPA of Kenya winning the Award for Excellence in Sustainable Finance, Banco Santander taking the Sustainable Global Bank of the Year transaction prize, and Impax Asset Management of the UK recognized as Sustainable Investor of the Year.[1]

HSBC Global Connections

The banking community is working to assist businesses in international development. HSBC Global Connections is an excellent website resource (www.globalconnections.hsbc.com) addressing risk management, supply chain, talent management, sustainability, and many more topics.

Netafim

One of the stories HSBC reported on is a company called Netafim, headquartered in Israel. This country is more home to subsidiaries rather than head offices, as Israel is not an easy country for people to export products from, due to its isolation.

This company has a great story of collaboration, innovation, and a vision of helping others by "growing more with less." It met the vision of Prime Minister David Ben-Gurion to "make the desert bloom." Netafim was a collaboration of a small kibbutz named Hazerim in the Negev desert with water engineer Simcha Blass.

Blass's innovation utilized a drip-based tube that slowly released water, which leads to amazing plant growth. This device is utilized in irrigation products around the world in more than 110 countries.

In 2011 Netafim saw growth of 30 percent worldwide, especially in emerging markets, such as India (where seed cotton yield was boosted by 85 percent, using 40 percent less water), Latin America, and Eastern Europe.

The comment that struck me the most about this company was this quote from the article: "We view each challenge through the eyes of our customers. We provide state-of-the-art technology, international agronomic expertise, and effective capacity-building training." This is one of the first principles of a quality management system—ISO 9000: "Organizations depend on their customers and therefore should understand current and future customer needs, meet customer requirements and strive to exceed customer expectations."

The principle from ISO 9000—"involvement of people—people at all levels is the essence of an organization and their full involvement enables their abilities to be used for the organization's benefit"—is followed by Netafim.

The organization grew through its own subsidiaries, not acquiring foreign businesses. What is interesting is how it operates in these areas. The CEO in India is Indian, and in the United States is American. The HSBC article "Sustainability—a Growth Strategy" quoted the company as saying, "We have a different culture in each subsidiary. We aim to understand their needs and limitations, and not force them to act in ways that are not reasonable in their countries."

These stories help us to see that growth and sustainability of one's business start with the principles the business works with and with the focus being on the customer.

Suncor's Challenge—"What Yes Can Do"—Our Voice

Industry plays a very important role in supporting communities, and many companies have done excellent work to help communities be self-sufficient and sustainable. In the beginning of the book, I spoke about leaders being those who ask questions and the need to be innovative.

The approach Suncor has taken is innovative, using video and the web to inform its viewers what it is doing to make a difference, under

"What Yes Can Do."[2] It has outlined its voice on how it is making a difference, sharing this information to teach, lead, and work together to make a difference (see Table 3.1).

TABLE 3.1	
Together, Let's See "What Yes Can Do"	
Environment	Can we raise the bar on environmental performance?
Innovation	Can we be leaders in Innovation?
Social	Can we help make communities stronger, self-sufficient, and sustainable?
Economic	Can we help sustain our quality of life and build our future?
People	Can we be concerned about the environment and work for an energy company?

Assess & Reflect #3

WHAT CAN "YES" DO AT OUR BUSINESS?

_____

_____

_____

_____

_____

_____

_____

_____

_____

_____

_____

_____

_____

_____

_____

_____

_____

_____

_____

_____

_____

_____

_____

Notes

1. Details can be found at www.ft-live.com/sustainablefinance.
2. Suncor website, www.suncor.com.

CHAPTER 4

International Institute for Sustainable Development

Drivers Pushing Business to Corporate Responsibility

The International Institute for Sustainable Development (IISD) has indicated that some of the drivers for pushing business to incorporate social responsibility (CSR) are as follows:

- The shrinking role of government leading to voluntary and non-regulatory initiatives
- Stakeholder demands for greater disclosure
- Increased customer interest in social performance of companies and its influence on their purchasing decisions
- Investor assessment of companies' performance based on criteria that now includes ethical concerns when buying and selling stocks
- Competitive labor markets—employees looking beyond paychecks and benefits to operating practices and principles; companies being forced to improve working conditions
- Supplier relations—ensuring that other companies' policies or practices do not tarnish your reputation

When an organization adopts a policy of social responsibility, some of the positive benefits can be: enhanced brand image and reputation, increased sales and customer loyalty, more ability to attract and retain employees, and improved operating costs and financial performance bringing access to capital.[1]

Global Reporting Initiative

The Global Reporting Initiative (GRI) is an international nonprofit organization, based in Amsterdam, the Netherlands, with a mission to make sustainability reporting standard practice for all companies and organizations, and produce sustainable reporting guidance.

GRI has Focal Point regional offices in Australia, Brazil, China, India, South Africa, and the United States. It has strategic partnerships with the United Nations Environment Programme, the UN Global Compact, the Organisation for Economic Co-operation and Development, the International Organization for Standardization, and others. It was founded in Boston in 1997 with its roots in the U.S. nonprofit organizations the Coalition for Environmentally Responsible Economies (CERES) and the Tellus Institute.

Its Sustainability Reporting Framework, used by thousands of organizations of all sizes and sectors, includes reporting guidelines, sector guidance, technical guidance, and other resources to provide greater organizational transparency and accountability. The first version was launched in 2000 and the fourth generation, Guidelines G4, in May 2013.

The reporting includes information about improving an organization's commitment to sustainable development for economic, environmental, social, and governance performance. The GRI Sustainability Reporting Guidelines allow organizations around the world to assess their sustainability performance and disclose the results in the same way as financial reporting.

GRI's annual report for 2012 indicated that 95 percent of the 250 biggest companies in the world report their sustainability performance, with 80 percent using the GRI Guidelines, according to an international study released by KPMG in November 2011.[2]

Corporate Responsibility Reporting

The KPMG Survey of Corporate Responsibility (CR) Reporting 2013 covers 4,100 companies in 41 countries, doing a report among the world's largest 250 companies, and it is the eighth edition of the report. The survey provides a snapshot of current global trends in corporate reporting and insights to help companies improve the quality of their reports.

The report stated that companies should no longer ask whether they should publish a CR report. With the high rate of CR reporting in all regions, it is now standard business practice worldwide.

Governments and stock exchanges around the world are now imposing mandatory reporting, and therefore the reporting is moving from a voluntary approach. The KPMG survey reported that more companies than ever are referring to the GRI guidelines in CR reporting.

A review was done on the G250 companies' reports and found that the quality of reporting was inconsistent. The following ten companies received high scores in demonstrating a superior understanding of the impact of social and environmental issues on their business and reported on their strategy, performance, and interaction with stakeholders.

- A.P. Møller Mærsk, Transport, Denmark
- BMW, Automotive, Germany
- Cisco Systems, Telecommunications and media, United States
- Ford Motor Company, Automotive, United States
- Hewlett Packard, Electronics and computers, United States
- ING Finance, Insurance and securities, The Netherlands
- Nestlé, Food and beverage, Switzerland
- Repsol, Oil and gas, Spain
- Siemens, Electronics and computers, Germany
- Total, Oil and gas, France

Lessons from the Leaders

KPMG reported the following from its interviews with leaders:

- Establish robust systems and processes for collecting data and identifying material issues: They reported that there is no "one-size-fits-all" solution for collecting data, as many of the companies developed their own solutions, rather than buying off-the-shelf products.

- Governance: Board-level commitment, management of sustainability on a day-to-day basis; reporting to board. Linking sustainability performance to remuneration.
- Lead from the front: Leaders need to be engaged and committed to CR.
- Create ownership: An example given was Vale, which engages 1,000 employees every year in producing its report.
- Reporting framework: Following the GR4 reporting framework.
- Understand social and environmental mega-forces and how they impact business: Be alert to commercial risks and opportunities.
- Materiality Process: Identify and prioritize actions.
- Targets and indicators are critical in order to improve: Set performance targets for sustainability time, bound with clear baseline and end date, measure progress, be transparent on performance.
- Management of suppliers and value chain: Identify risks in supply chain and systems for managing them.
- Stakeholder engagement: Identify and engage key stakeholders, responding to feedback and taking action.
- Transparency and balance: Acknowledge challenges, dilemmas, failures, achievements, and monitor performance, making it available to stakeholders.[3]

Future trends that were discussed in the report by these leaders include: integration of CR reporting with financial reporting; communication around CR more frequently in the future (e.g., publishing a half-yearly CR performance report or an update as events occur); and an evolution of reporting to include local-level reporting, employees, and external local stakeholders.

Assess & Reflect #4

LESSONS FROM LEADERS ON SUSTAINABILITY:
WHAT ARE OUR LESSONS LEARNED ON SUSTAINABILITY?

_____

_____

_____

_____

_____

_____

_____

_____

_____

_____

_____

_____

_____

_____

_____

_____

_____

_____

_____

_____

_____

_____

_____

_____

Notes

1. For further information on the Institute refer to its website at www.iisd.org/business/issues/sr.aspx.
2. Reports on corporate sustainability can be found on the United Nations Global Compact website, www.unglobalcompact.org.
3. For quotes from the leaders from these organizations and details, refer to the report (KPMG Survey of Corporate Responsibility (CR) Reporting 2013), which can be found on KPMG's website, or by contacting the Global Head of Sustainability Reporting & Assurance.

CHAPTER 5

Defining Business Sustainability

Today major fund managers want to have complete confidence that their capital is protected in an investment that is well managed, with a company's management being accountable for business performance.

SUSTAINABILITY

DOW JONES SUSTAINABILITY INDEX

a business approach that creates long-term shareholder value by embracing opportunities and managing risks deriving from economic, environmental and social developments.

Sustainability will require an organization to have the ability to manage its risks with the creation of strong business principles and international management system framework (quality, environment, health and safety) for business productivity, innovation, and success. The decisions made today will impact the success of the business, quality of life, and the meaningful future of our world.

Sustainable development as outlined on the International Institute for Sustainable Development website www.iisd.org is defined as "Environmental, economic and social well-being for today and tomorrow."

Business leaders need to think about their business as a part of our world's system, where business management interacts and impacts us all.

SUSTAINABILITY DEFINITION

Pilot's Definition of Sustainability

The ability to sustain business.

Source: Pilot Performance Resources Management Inc.

Definitions of Sustainability

The first step in having business success tied with sustainability is to determine your definition of sustainability.

Here are three definitions to consider. **What will be yours?**

1. UN: "Sustainability calls for a decent standard of living for everyone today without compromising the needs of future generations."
2. Dow Jones Sustainability: "A business approach that creates long-term shareholder value by embracing opportunities and managing risks deriving from economic, environmental and social developments."
3. Pilot Performance Resources Management Inc.: "The ability to sustain business."

Assess & Reflect #5

WHAT IS MY DEFINITION OF SUSTAINABILITY?

_____

_____

_____

_____

_____

_____

_____

_____

_____

_____

_____

_____

_____

_____

_____

_____

_____

_____

_____

_____

_____

_____

_____

Taking the Next Steps to Business Success

Business leaders take the first step for business success with the development of their business "principles," which will be outlined in Part II of this book, where you have the opportunity to assess, reflect, and act on your business principles. Part III will introduce you to management-system thinking, following Pilot's Three Steps.

Now is the time to act, building a resilient business–management system structure that can be integrated with collaboration of corporate strategies and corporate culture that will help your organization be successful and survive in the future.

System Thinking

Wikipedia defines system thinking as follows:

> System thinking is not one thing but a set of habits or practices within a framework that is based on the belief that the component parts of a system can best be understood in the context of relationships with each other and with other systems, rather than in isolation.

As a manager, director, and leader in the organization, you are the visionary who will make the future for the organization. Choices need to be made and urgency is upon you.

Changes in business are happening at an unbelievable speed, due to the Internet. The lives of individuals and businesses are interconnected around the world today.

Innovation and technology is a power that will keep you in the race.

Assess & Reflect #6

HOW WILL OUR FUTURE UNFOLD?

WHERE WILL OUR BUSINESS BE IN THE FUTURE, IN THE NEXT TWO TO THREE YEARS?

_____

_____

_____

_____

_____

_____

_____

_____

_____

_____

_____

_____

_____

_____

_____

_____

_____

_____

_____

Ready for the Coming Age of Abundance

The internet has been a medium that brings about innovation of change for businesses, linking them together to source information and services. Global access has brought about greater flexibility in working hours and location of businesses. Content management systems allow business personnel to work on shared documents simultaneously from different parts of the world. Educational material is available providing distance education.

Social networking websites like Facebook, Twitter, LinkedIn, and YouTube offer new ways to interact and communicate. Companies have new opportunities to market products and services.

YouTube Video—Innovators and Managers of Change

YouTube is viewed by billions of users, with over 6 billion hours of video being watched each month, which is almost an hour for every person on earth, as outlined on its statistics page.[1]

A video I would recommend managers watch is called "Are We Ready for the Coming 'Age of Abundance'?" which features the marvels of achievement and how the world has taken a quantum leap.[2] It starts with Gabriel Byrne talking about living in a world of profound change and how technology is defining and driving our world. He stresses the need to be prepared for this journey and the opportunities it will present.

The video is then moderated by Tom Stewart, Chief Marketing and Knowledge Officer of Booz & Company. He was the editor and managing director of *Harvard Business Review* and the pioneer of the concept of "intellectual capital," which he outlined in his book *The Wealth of Knowledge: Intellectual Capital and the Twenty-First Century Organization*.

The following four people speak about the future of business. They are true innovators and managers of change, working to make a difference in our world:

1. Dr. Michio Kaku, an internationally recognized physicist, best-selling author, and futurist of science. He is cofounder of the string field theory. His goal is to help complete Einstein's dream of a "theory of everything," a single equation that will unify all the fundamental forces in the universe.

2. Michael Schrage, MIT Sloan School of Digital Business, author of *Serious Play* and a new *Harvard Business Review* single, *Who Do You Want Your Customers to Become?*

3. Dr. Peter Diamandis, coauthor of *Abundance: The Future Is Better than You Think* and author of the forthcoming book *Bold*. He looks to technology and intelligence to solve life's challenges. He is chairman and CEO of X-Prize, which is leading innovation in the world by designing and launching large incentive prizes that are driving radical breakthroughs for the benefit of humanity. I love his quote: "The best way to predict the future is to create it yourself." He cofounded the Singularity University, a Silicon Valley institution with many partners from NASA, Google, Autodesk, and Nokia that will work with the world's top enterprises to utilize technology and incentive innovation to accelerate their business objectives.

4. Isabel Aguilera, an independent advisor for Indra Systems (flight simulators and weapons system training) and president of Twindocs. She is past president of GE in Spain and former CEO of Google Spain and Portugal. *Forbes Magazine* named her as one of the 50 most influential women in the world.

Three Areas That Will Affect and Improve Business

Three areas will affect and improve business, as outlined by the speakers:

1. Mobility (Internet, mobile devices)
2. The cloud
3. Instant analysis of data (for decision making—real-time data)

How you put these three areas in to use for the future will determine where you are in the race.

Assess & Reflect #7

WHAT WILL BE OUR TOP THREE BUSINESS CHALLENGES?

_____

_____

_____

_____

_____

_____

_____

_____

_____

_____

_____

_____

_____

_____

_____

_____

_____

_____

_____

_____

_____

_____

_____

Business Challenges: Management of Business Knowledge

> We cannot solve our problems with the same level of thinking that created them.
>
> *—Albert Einstein*

I support the concept that life gives us wings to explore and knowledge gives us power to create and evolve.

Two reasons we make mistakes in business are: (1) lack of information and (2) inexperience. Therefore, I am concerned with the following areas in the management of businesses today: data analysis, innovation, and the grey tsunami (baby boomer retirement, talent management and infrastructure deterioration).

Data Analysis

Firstly, the rate of change that is occurring in business requires companies to focus on data analysis for decision making, and change management to stay competitive and profitable in today's marketplace. Leadership needs to be strong to manage these changes, and management system structures need to be in place for the strategic initiatives that support the company's vision and operational controls.

Leaders need to transition to smart decisions that are data-driven. Businesses have not been good at managing data analysis and management of change in the past, and now with social media, they need to have information- and change-management processes in place to be able to make changes faster within the management system.

The company's management system structure is important to manage its processes for planning (branding—marketing—customer service—objectives—targets—financial—legal); implementation (communication—human resources—training—production—operational control); monitoring (nonconformances, audits); and evaluating data and performance improvement (management reviews).

The ability to acquire and analyze information with the use of social media, technology, cloud computing, and ERP systems will be necessary and is the primary responsibility of the CEO.

Employees across the organization will need to use data analysis and management of change processes in the course of their work in: strategic decision making, operational efficiency, financial controlling, customer service satisfaction and account management, regulatory compliance, and market and business development. These areas will be addressed in more detail later.

Innovation

Secondly, getting and recognizing input from employees is needed for innovation. Skill shortages will cause companies to lose employees to companies that recognize and support them.

Innovation can be defined as an original or new breakthrough idea, something different in your products, services, processes, and technology, or something that gives your organization a foothold in the marketplace.

Considering this definition, it is imperative to look at innovation and ask what value this innovation provides to your customer, or how it improves your customer's satisfaction.

Grey Tsunami—Talent Management

Thirdly, the drain of knowledge and know-how of baby boomer managers, as many will be leaving the workforce through retirement, will affect your sustainability. I call this the grey tsunami. If not captured before they leave your organization, the lack of this information or know-how could have a huge impact on the success of your organization. Succession planning is crucial now. Do you know how many people will be leaving your organization in the next year or three to five years?

Having a management system structure (data management) in place to capture these managers' know-how is critical. The time to act is now, by acquiring and documenting in your management system structure their know-how.

Mentoring programs would also assist in this transition. Bringing in the young to work with the old assists in the turnover; however, the young think differently than the old. This will provide a new approach to the way business will be done in the future.

Boston Consulting Group

The Boston Consulting Group (BCG), a global private management consulting firm with 81 offices in 45 countries, is one of the leading advisors on business strategy, helping clients achieve sustainable competitive advantage since 1963. In December 2013 it issued a press release entitled "Talent Management and Digital Readiness Are among Most Significant Blind Spots, Says a Global Survey of Business Leaders."

It is interesting to note that it found that "business leaders around the world felt least prepared to execute on strategies for driving growth— among them, large-scale transformation, open innovation, digital channels and talent management—according to a global survey they released which included 1,000 senior executives from different sectors and regions."[3]

Notes

1. YouTube's statistics page is available at www.youtube.com/yt/press/statistics.html.
2. "Are We Ready For the Coming 'Age of Abundance?'" by Dr. Michio Kaku. Available at www.youtube.com/watch?v=ceEog1XS5OI.
3. Details on the survey can be obtained by viewing the media release at www.bcg.com/media.

Principles for Driving Business Success

Managers have taken on a worldwide vision to retain a competitive edge in today's global business environment, leveraging business sustainability to provide a better return on investment and improved business performance, and managing risks. As outlined in Part I, CEOs need to see business value, as they are the architects of their business world.

How will you as a manager and a leader measure up during this time?

What is business sustainability? My definition, as stated in Part I, is the "ability to sustain business" or investing now for future business success. To do this, you as a leader or manager require excellent business principles and process management system thinking to collaborate and integrate corporate strategies and culture to fulfill your business mission. Thinking only of environmental and social sustainability does not give the value of success and survival to the organization, as outlined in Part I of the book. You need to look at your business principles and management system structure as applicable to quality, environment, health and safety and financial performance, your bottom line.

What will be your business challenges? One will be the grey tsunami—the management of your talent pool. Will you allow this to be a ripple or a tidal wave? Action is needed now.

In the next 5 to 10 years, one third of our population will be retiring and with them go aging managers and knowledge management of business operations, which I refer to as the grey tsunami. With the replacement of the old with the new managers, will the principles of business still be the same? This is yet to be determined; however, I don't believe so.

The grey tsunami also refers to the deterioration of our infrastructure: roads, bridges, and underground piping, which was built by our forefathers and has not been monitored for repairs and replacements. This will have an indirect effect on your business dealing with transportation of your goods or the manufacturing of them, but will also provide opportunities for business. Have you looked at these challenges or opportunities within your business?

Other challenges will be globalization, process integration, management of intelligence and resources, and automation of data.

Business leaders need to define their core values in terms of principles that their organization will follow to conduct activities and make vital business decisions, while carrying out their vision and mission for success.

Many times we hear that failure is due to lack of financial resources, but possibly it is due to a lack of focus or creativity in managing business principles, or a dysfunctional business structure for management and measurement of not only your processes but also of data for fulfillment of your vision.

Principles for Management Systems

Management principles outline the essential correct code of conduct, as well as essential characteristics for effective and efficient operation of a management system to produce necessary outcomes for business success and survival. These principles will assist managers in creating a successful business culture to improve their organization's performance.

All successful managers follow principles that they value, which help define the purpose and direction of their business performance.

Asking, Not Telling

A leader is one who asks thought-provoking business questions, who is open-minded, focusing on feasible solutions and not on interrogating team players. By asking questions, managers can get different insights into opportunities for improving the management of their businesses. Success or the growth of a company is more about asking than telling. This leads to what I refer to as "Management System Makeovers™."

Managers need to take the time to "Assess" and "Reflect" on their principles. This section on principles provides questions top management can ask themselves, as well as their management team and customers, and is an opportunity to seek clarification about the principles of operating their business.

Do your values align with international thinking? Before presenting the questions outlined in the "Assess & Reflect" sections to your management team, determine the order of priority that works best for your organization and the addition of any relevant questions for your company.

I refer to principles as having the five Ps: possibilities, priorities, performance, productivity, and profits. When businesses can think divergently and be innovative with a team approach, the world is their oyster.

Part II will teach business leaders to understand and fulfill the needs of their customers, as customer satisfaction will ensure the success of a company. The international standard applicable to customer satisfaction is ISO 9001 in quality management.

This part refers to principles for quality, environment, and health, and safety with a summary of integrated principles for a business management system. It also addresses the benefits of having a management system structure in place that meets international standards for global trade.

CHAPTER 6

Principles for Quality Management Systems

G ood managers or leaders are team builders, known by their integrity, substance, and character. These managers know the needs of their customers and can empower their employees, aligning their direction with common goals to improve process operations for ultimate performance.

People who are employed by the organization are looking for meaning and stability; they are willing to put in the effort to make the difference if the work environment is supportive. This allows their creativity and input to support the passion and purpose of their management to serve customers better than competitors.

Financial management helps the company maintain control, but a company looking for business success and survival will succeed only when the management system framework is in place to support its processes. The ISO 9001 international standard for quality helps a company align its mission and dedication to serve its customers with superior products or services and manage effectively and efficiently.

Since 1994, I have supported international standards for management systems, as the business management structure is one that is understood around the world; when you are doing business globally, you need to all play on a level playing field. Management system frameworks, however, are only as good as the supported government legislation for compliance tied with environmental, health, and safety issues.

The three main international management system standards that many companies are registered to or can self-declare their management system to are: Quality Management Systems—ISO 9001, Environmental Management Systems—ISO 14001, and the Occupational Health & Safety Assessment Scheme—OHSAS 18001.

These standards are applicable to any organization, small or large, whatever its product or service. To manage business today, three different management systems are not necessary. Integrated management systems reduce duplication and streamline your business for success. The new generic framework, which will be discussed in Part III, will assist in this development.

The International Organization for Standardization (ISO) through its ISO Technical Committee, ISO/TC 176 on Quality, came up with quality management principles, as defined in ISO 9000, "Quality management systems—fundamentals and vocabulary," and in ISO 9004, "Managing for the sustained success of an organization—a quality management approach."

We have outlined these quoted principles in this chapter. These principles are derived from collective experience and knowledge from the international experts who participate in the technical ISO committee. They can be used as a basis for performance improvement in your business, driving business success and survival.[1]

Customer Focus

Organizations depend on their customers and therefore should understand current and future customer needs, should meet customer requirements, and strive to exceed customer expectations.

Without customers, your business would not exist. Your business success is determined by your customers' satisfaction. Your customer

QUALITY PRINCIPLES

Quality Management System Principles

- Customer focus
- Leadership
- Involvement of people
- Process approach
- System approach to management
- Continual improvement
- Factual approach to decision making
- Mutually beneficial supplier relationships

might be your corporate head office or it might be hundreds of clients. It is vital to identify who your customers are.

By identifying your customers' requirements, now and for the future, striving to meet and exceed their expectations, you work proactively to improve customer loyalty and sustain or increase revenue, benefiting both your organization and your customers.

Top management ensures that customer-related processes are implemented in its management system structure to determine customer requirements for order processing, and any amendments through delivery and postdelivery requirements (warranty, contractual obligations, such as maintenance services, and supplementary services, such as recycling and disposal).

The focus needs to be on building strong customer relationships, understanding their needs, and providing "value" for what they are paying. Customer retention is good business sense as it costs more to bring in new business than it does to maintain the relationships that you have built. Long-term customers are happy to share the good qualities of your organization.

All employees need to understand the importance and focus of customer satisfaction and their role in representing the company to the customer. Appropriate, effective handling of customer feedback, including customer complaints, helps to maintain customer satisfaction, allowing employees to realize that what they say or do reflects on the company. Today in the age of social media, it is so easy for customers to voice their concerns publicly through the web (Twitter, Facebook, YouTube), which could have a negative impact on the company.

Communication is vital to customer satisfaction. Building customer loyalty involves not only dealing with customer complaints but also keeping your customers informed about your product or service.

CUSTOMER FOCUS

FOCUS: QUALITY—CUSTOMER

1. What are you doing to work with your customers? Does your company put customers at the center of making business decisions? How?
2. Is your company rated by outside market-research firms for delivering superior customer service? What is your rating?
3. Who are your target client/s? Who are your top ten clients?
4. What do you need to know about your customers?
5. How has your organization demonstrated excellence in building relationships with your customers?
6. What are you doing to improve customer loyalty?
7. What systems are in place to understand existing and potential customers' needs and their expectations?
8. Speed is of the essence. Is your company able to seize market opportunities as they happen? Why or why not?
9. How do you deal with customer expectations that are not being met?
10. Are objectives of the organization linked to customer need, satisfaction, and expectation?
11. How do you communicate with customers (written, verbal, Internet/social media)?
12. How are customers' needs communicated throughout the organization and with other stakeholders?
13. What systems are in place for tracking customer needs, customer problems, and customer satisfaction?
    a. Do your employees (workers) offer solutions to make your customer happy?
    b. Do you keep records of actions taken?
    c. Do you manage problems through your nonconformance system?
14. When a customer requests a feature for a product or service that your company does not provide, what do employees tell the customer? Do they give alternatives?

(continued)

Asses & Reflect (continued)

15 What do you monitor and measure to track and maintain high levels of customer satisfaction?
   a. Timely delivery of products or services
   b. Quality of product/service delivered, easy to use
   c. Support services: Timeliness
   d. Warranties
   e. Customer loyalty: Repeat business
   f. Other

16 Have there been any changes to existing procedures or work instructions in order to increase customer satisfaction metrics? What were they?
   a. How do you get input to make changes in procedures?
   b. How do you manage communicating these changes to others and getting their support?
   c. How do you track or measure the outcome of this change?

Act

CUSTOMER FOCUS

FOCUS: QUALITY—CUSTOMER

_____

_____

_____

_____

_____

_____

_____

_____

_____

_____

_____

_____

_____

_____

_____

_____

_____

_____

_____

_____

_____

_____

_____

_____

_____

_____

_____

Leadership

Leaders establish unity of purpose and direction of the organization. They should create and maintain the internal environment in which people can become fully involved in achieving the organization's objectives.

Top management of an organization, whether the president, CEO, general manager, or owner, needs to establish unity of purpose and direction for the organization, so that all interested parties, including customers, owners, employees, contractors, suppliers, and financial people, can become fully involved in achieving the organization's mission for its future.

Management needs to be purposeful and results-oriented for quality and continual improvement; therefore, change management is a key part of leadership.

Leaders influence and motivate others. Top managers have made a commitment to implement a quality management system following international standards and their own requirements, as well as to meet statutory and regulatory requirements.

When making this commitment, top management needs to ensure availability of resources and training, ensuring that responsibilities, accountability, and competencies are defined and communicated. Managers need to lead by example, inspiring and encouraging others and recognizing employee contributions.

The board of directors needs to be aware of the operational risks tied not only with quality but also with environment, health, and safety. It is important that the board approves the management system framework and be kept informed of identified risks and how they are controlled, monitored, and measured. This helps the board know about risk areas and what can impact performance and profits. Shareholders want to invest in companies that grow and manage their risks by putting in controls for success.

Managers conduct management reviews to understand the status of the management system and provide ongoing direction for the continual improvement of the effectiveness of its management system. Records outlining inputs and outputs of the management reviews provide the support for due diligence.

Two reasons we make mistakes in life are 1) lack of information and 2) inexperience. Asking questions helps us to be proactive and to gather the information to make better decisions and take better directions.

LEADERSHIP

FOCUS: QUALITY—CUSTOMER

1 What is the purpose of your company being in business?
  a. What is the vision for the company for the next three to five years?
  b. What are you contributing to customers, to society?
  c. What is unique about your company? What makes you different from your competitor? Does your branding reflect this?

2 How do you want to be remembered as a manager or leader of your organization? What values (principles) do you have for the company?

3 What can or will impact the success of your business?

4 What tools does your company have in place to translate the skills of leadership effectiveness and outcomes into metrics?
  a. Internal: Company performance—KPI (key performance indicators)—financial
  b. External: Business awards

5 Interested parties for unity of purpose: Customers, employees, suppliers, contractors, shareholders, community, etc.
  a. What and how does the organization communicate as a clear vision to these people related to its management system's vision, policy, and strategic planning objectives?
  b. How do vision, policy, and objectives impact interested parties?
  c. How can you best serve your shareholders and your customers?
  d. How can you engage your employees, contractors, and suppliers?
  e. What input do interested parties have in the company's direction? What innovative changes have been made?
  f. How is recognition given to interested parties for their contributions and encouragement given for continual improvement?

6 How do you as a manager communicate to employees the importance of meeting and continually improving customer satisfaction? Are you as a manager listening?

    a. Does your organization have customer focus groups?

    b. Employee-customer feedback sessions?

7 How does your organization communicate to employees the importance of meeting corporate and legal requirements?

8 Planning

    a. What three objectives do you have in place for quality?

    b. What is the status of them? Do you as an owner, general manager, or president attend management meetings to check the status? (Is your attendance at any of these meeting unannounced?)

    c. How are ongoing objectives or projects tracked at your organization?

9 How does the organization capture internal change management?

10 Recognition

    a. When employees exceed goals, how are they recognized?

    b. Do you recognize customer service? How—awards, congratulations?

11 Do management reviews show that the quality management system is effective and improving?

12 Are you accessible to employees and other managers? Are you engaged with your employees?

Act

LEADERSHIP

FOCUS: QUALITY—CUSTOMER

_____

_____

_____

_____

_____

_____

_____

_____

_____

_____

_____

_____

_____

_____

_____

_____

_____

_____

_____

_____

_____

_____

_____

_____

_____

_____

Involvement of People

People at all levels are the essence of an organization and their full involvement enables their abilities to be used for the organization's benefit.

A company's strength is not only its customers but also the people who were chosen to work with the organization. How top management has organized and involved its people will determine their input and participation. Keeping track of real-time involvement in projects is key in managing one's business. Today, visibility and an integrated management system, allows you to better allocate your resources, stay within budget, and manage your business for profitability.

The organization focuses on people by defining roles and responsibilities; however, it is important that they take ownership and are emotionally engaged so that they feel they can actively contribute and make improvements. By ignoring the emotional engagement, companies will be missing out on the financial returns, as productivity decreases and input is not supporting the direction of the organization.

Partnerships are everything. Individuals need to be a part of a team so that sharing of knowledge, skills, and experiences can take place. They need the understanding of how their work can add value for customers and support the organization's goals, aligning a partnership for performance to work toward customer satisfaction. Employees not only accomplish tasks to assist in customer satisfaction but also set the tone for the customer's perception of how they are treated (positively or negatively), and they use their knowledge when giving advice to a customer, which could provide added value in the customer relationship, increasing customer satisfaction.

A team approach ensures that everyone is equal and working toward the same goals and objectives and that the participants understand what is expected. They need to feel free to express their ideas and concepts and trust each other in order for the team approach to be satisfying and rewarding. Disagreement within the team is productive as it brings out other options to consider. Processes need to be in place to resolve conflict and provide clarity to move forward. This may be accomplished by consensus or by the team leader making the ultimate decision on directions to take.

Employees need to see progress in their own growth, as an individual and within an organization; otherwise they will look to other opportunities. As mentioned earlier in this chapter, many employees will be retiring in the next five to ten years, and an organization needs to have in place a way to capture the knowledge that key personnel have related to the organization's operations, and a plan to bring new personnel in to be trained prior to their leaving.

Assess & Reflect #10

INVOLVEMENT OF PEOPLE

FOCUS: QUALITY—CUSTOMER

1 How does the organization promote innovation and empower its people to contribute to meeting the organization's goals? Do you reward them? How?

2 How does top management as leaders for the organization assist employees and contractors to understand the importance of their contribution and to get satisfaction from their work (defining expectations, career development, stable employment, job design)?

3 Are people passionate and proud to be a part of your organization? How do they show this? Will the organization maintain human resources?

4 Does the organization have a plan in place to capture the knowledge of employees retiring in the near future? How will it manage the selection of new employees to replace these people? Has it analyzed how many people will be retiring within the organization and when?

5 Does the organization evaluate employee performance against personal goals and objectives? How often? How?

6 Do personnel work together in "work teams"? Does the organization promote "champions"? How?

7 Does the organization motivate its people by focusing on their strengths or does it focus on improving weaknesses?

8 Do interested parties share their knowledge and experience? Do they openly discuss problems or issues? How are they followed up?

9 How does the organization support innovation?

10 How does the company track real-time involvement of its people in projects?

Act

INVOLVEMENT OF PEOPLE

Focus: Quality—Customer

_____

_____

_____

_____

_____

_____

_____

_____

_____

_____

_____

_____

_____

_____

_____

_____

_____

_____

_____

_____

_____

_____

_____

_____

Process Approach

A desired result is achieved more efficiently when activities and related resources are managed as a process.

The term *process* is defined as a set of interrelated or interacting activities that transforms inputs into outputs.

Wikipedia outlines process management as "the management of the application of knowledge, skills, tools, techniques and systems to define, visualize, measure, control, report and improve processes with the goal to meet customer requirements profitably. ISO 9001 promotes the process approach to managing an organization."

By creating process maps, a company can follow a process approach to managing its business. By identifying a company's processes, its interrelationships and associated risks provide transparency. A process approach can be used not only for a quality management system but also for other systems, such as environment and health and safety. This will help an organization focus its efforts on its processes' effectiveness and efficiency and its management of risks.

Utilizing a process approach can lower costs through focusing on prioritizing performance improvement activities for each process, thereby ensuring effective use of resources tied with risks, and achieving desired outcomes.

The organization will need to identify and determine the sequence and interaction of its processes. This may, depending on the scope, be for the entire organization, a business unit, a department, or an individual area. As part of this identification, it is essential to determine the inputs and outputs for its processes by a team that is familiar with the process. An output from one process can be an input into another. Evaluate possible risks and consequences tied with each process that could impact customers, suppliers, or other stakeholders.

By process mapping, you can review the workflow through a model or pictures of activities that take place in the process and see if there are any omissions, incomplete documented operating procedures, lack of training for a process, or any redundancies or duplication. You can view resource allocations to see if accountability is tied to the process and see the interaction of those involved, as well as the competencies required.

The organization would then determine the criteria and methods needed to ensure operation and control of processes, ensuring availability of resources. Each process needs to be monitored and measured, where applicable, and analyzed so that actions are taken to continually improve.

Process mapping assists in document management, not only procedures developed for operational control but also records maintained.

Typical processes as outlined in an ISO 9001 management system model may include the following; however, every organization has unique processes that would need to be identified, rather than a hierarchy of functions:

1. **Management processes**
   a. Planning (strategic to manage risks, opportunities, continual improvement), leadership, policies, objectives, legality, change management, management review
2. **Support processes**
   a. Quality assurance, environment, health and safety, emergency
   b. Resources—human, infrastructure, training
   c. Financial
   d. Information system support—IT
   e. Maintenance and facility management
3. **Business realization processes (operational planning and control)**
   a. Marketing
   b. Sales
   c. Order processing
   d. Design and development
   e. Material control (supply chain), purchasing, receiving/shipping, inventory, warehousing
   f. Production and service

4. Continual improvement processes—performance evaluation

 a. Customer satisfaction

 b. Management system (MS) processes

  i. Audits—internal and registration

  ii. Monitoring and measurement

   • Analysis—evaluation

   • Improvement

  iii. Nonconformity and corrective actions

  iv. Compliance

 c. Product

  i. Inspection and test

  ii. Verification/validation

PROCESS APPROACH

Focus: Quality—Customer

1. Have processes been defined? How (matrix, flowchart, mapping)? Have interfaces of key activities between the functions of the organization been identified? What are they?
2. Did you perform process mapping? Did you find duplication or omissions of activities?
3. Have process owners been defined? Does the management team include all the process owners?
4. What are the inputs and outputs for these processes? Has identification of customers', suppliers', and other interested parties' requirements been made for each process? Has the organization outlined activities necessary to obtain a desired output from the process?
5. Have risks been defined for the processes?
6. Has your organization identified the criteria and methods needed to ensure that both the operation and control of these processes are effective?
7. Do you analyze and measure the capability of key activities for the processes?
8. What areas were identified for process improvement?
   a. Reducing cost and cycle time
   b. Increasing profits
   c. Increasing performance
   d. Accelerating schedules
   e. Providing training
   f. Improving customer satisfaction
9. What outcomes would add value to the organization? What strategic plans or performance objectives have been defined to oversee the organization's mission and improve customer satisfaction?
10. What budget allocations are necessary to support process changes?

Act

PROCESS APPROACH

FOCUS: QUALITY—CUSTOMER

_____

_____

_____

_____

_____

_____

_____

_____

_____

_____

_____

_____

_____

_____

_____

_____

_____

_____

_____

_____

_____

_____

_____

_____

_____

_____

System Approach to Management

Identifying, understanding and managing interrelated processes as a system contributes to the organization's effectiveness and efficiency in achieving its objectives.

By having a system approach to management, you will identify and understand how your processes interrelate and how their interdependencies contribute to the effectiveness and efficiency in meeting the organization's objectives and meeting customer satisfaction.

Companies are usually structured in a hierarchy of functional units, and therefore in many functions, the customer is not always considered in managing their area(s). Their focus is on the goals tied to the functional area and not the output related to "customer satisfaction," which is the focus of the system approach.

ISO 9001 promotes the process approach to quality management in order to function effectively by managing linked activities in order to enable transformation of inputs into outputs. In many cases the output from one process forms the input into the next.

In a system approach you can follow Pilot Performance's Three-Step Process—Identify, Insure, Improve™, which is discussed in Part III, "Integrated Management System Implementation."

Assess & Reflect #12

SYSTEM APPROACH TO MANAGEMENT

Focus: Quality—Customer

1. What criteria do you manage your business to?
2. Do you do business internationally? Have you been asked if your business has international standards of management systems in place, such as ISO 9001, ISO 14001, or OHSAS 18001?
3. How do you manage your linked business activities?
   a. Business units
   b. Process system approach
   c. Other
4. Are processes improving? How does management know?
5. What processes are used for determining this?
6. Does your organization understand organizational capabilities and resource constraints prior to action?
7. What measurement and evaluation do you have in place in your management system?
8. How has the organization met its business needs through technology—for example, automation of business functions?
9. Has the management system supported the company's vision?
10. Is the company "walking the talk" (doing what you say you are doing)?
11. How do you control management of your business documentation? Does your quality manual make reference to your processes and applicable linkages with procedures and software programs managing your process areas for ease in capturing knowledge management?
12. What controlled conditions are in place for production and service provision? Does your organization work with quality control plans that outline characteristics and controls?
13. What systems do you have in place for the validation of processes for production and service provision? What systems are in place for identification and traceability throughout product/service realization?

Act

SYSTEM APPROACH TO MANAGEMENT

FOCUS: QUALITY—CUSTOMER

_____

_____

_____

_____

_____

_____

_____

_____

_____

_____

_____

_____

_____

_____

_____

_____

_____

_____

_____

_____

_____

_____

_____

_____

_____

Continual Improvement

Continual improvement of the organization's overall performance should be a permanent objective of the organization.

Continual improvement should lead a company to enhance performance, productivity, and profits, as well as customer and stakeholder satisfaction on an ongoing basis. Continual improvement requires management to support innovation and excellence.

We can look to continual improvement and monitoring and measurement for performance in three areas: (1) quality management system, (2) conformity of product/service requirements, and (3) customer satisfaction. Pilot's Three-Step Process: Identify, Insure, Improve™ can be used in this process. Step One is to identify your current performance tied to quality management, reviewing your strategic planning initiatives. Establish a need and then get the commitment to establish objectives. Ensure that you have the research or analysis correct in order to proceed to establish projects or programs to support the objectives. An important technique for improving a process is to look at value analysis. Is there value added or nonvalue added by the activities performed? It is strategic to put in place key process improvement strategies that are measureable, and tied to your financials to see the value to the success of the organization's profitability.

Many organizations put in place key performance indicators (KPIs); however, are they doing this to show measurement for receiving their ISO registration or are they setting objectives to improve process improvements? Has the organization really improved its processes? What gets measured gets done.

Step Two is to insure. Active participation and buy-in from all parties tied with the organization's change is needed to achieve continual improvement of the organization's performance. It is important to recognize what activities are being performed by whom, how, and when.

When proper controls and measurement are in place, analysis and trending can be accurately done, showing where improvement needs to be focused now and in the future.

As continual improvement is an ongoing process for the company, it is important to have structure in place to manage this process. The setting of objectives throughout the organization is important for improvement and management of what is taking place at the organization. I have been in many companies where managers are working on many projects, and there is not one location that managers can go to view what is being worked on by whom.

In order for top management to know what is going on in their organization, they need to understand what each process area is working on; otherwise, people are just being busy and not concentrating on meeting the main goals of the company. The management of workloads can be automated to a central location working with your IT department.

One of the measurements of the performance of the quality management system is in Step Three, improvement that reviews the monitoring of customer's perception of whether the organization has met customer requirements, which is the measurement of customer satisfaction. This can be done through customer surveys, customer data, repeat business or lost business analysis, warranty claims, or dealer reports, to name a few methods.

For an understanding of how the company's management system is improving or not, this can be managed by monitoring and measuring processes and products, as well as verified through the internal audit program. The organization needs to have trained competent auditors who are objective and impartial about the area they are auditing to provide reporting on meeting management system criteria. Any nonconformances to the management system or noncompliance with legal requirements need to be processed through your nonconformance process. Having one process to handle all nonconformances, assists in understanding all the deficiencies and the priorities required to each. The nonconformances can be categorized for easy evaluation.

Management responsible for the area being found to have nonconformance/noncompliance is to ensure that root causes are evaluated and that necessary corrections or corrective actions are taken without any undue delay. Records of the monitoring, measurement, and audits need to be maintained.

Assess & Reflect #13

CONTINUAL IMPROVEMENT

FOCUS: QUALITY—CUSTOMER

1. In what areas have you improved the effectiveness of your management system in the last three months, six months, and year?
2. How do you as a manager encourage continual improvement within the organization?
3. Who within your organization is responsible for continual improvement?
4. Has the organization made the continual improvement of products, processes, and systems an objective for every individual in the organization?
5. What tools are used to assist in continual improvement (policy statement, objectives and targets, Six Sigma, Lean, SWOT analysis, brainstorming, storyboarding, value analysis, trend analysis, change management, project management, internal and third-party audits, corrective and preventive action, root cause analysis, management reviews)?
6. How does the organization know if it is improving? Is work being done per improvement plan (objectives/targets)? Does the organization measure its improvements? Is it testing solutions? Does it make adjustments going forward?
    a. Does the organization have higher customer satisfaction?
    b. Has the organization increased productivity?
    c. Are people spending less time and incurring fewer costs to perform activities?
    d. Are managers able to expand organizational capabilities?
    e. Has the organization reduced "re" in quality—*rework, reschedule, resubmit*?
7. How does management ensure that the program or project worked on for continual improvement is rolled into the management system (operational controls in place, training provided, competent personnel, etc.)?
8. How do you recognize and acknowledge improvements?

(continued)

Asses & Reflect (continued)

(9) How will newly defined objectives support the company's guiding principles?

(10) What have your internal and third-party audits assisted in improving? Is your organization continuing to learn more about its processes and its management system?

(11) How is change management viewed at your organization? Is the management system improvement looked at as building a stronger, successful company by your employees? (Why do most people resist change?)

Act

CONTINUAL IMPROVEMENT

FOCUS: QUALITY—CUSTOMER

_____
_____
_____
_____
_____
_____
_____
_____
_____
_____
_____
_____
_____
_____
_____
_____
_____
_____
_____
_____
_____
_____
_____
_____
_____
_____
_____
_____
_____

Factual Approach to Decision Making

Effective decisions are based on the analysis of data and information.

In order to make informed decisions, it is imperative to have data and information that are accurate and reliable, and provided easily for those who require it. Personnel need to be in a position, or have the authority to make decisions and take appropriate actions, based on outcomes of factual analysis, balanced with knowledge, experience in interpreting information, and insight.

Emphasis is put on top management to outline its commitment to quality in a quality policy statement, and it is supported by management system reviews. Decisions are made at these reviews as to the effectiveness and efficiency of managing the organization's performance.

Inputs for these reviews are from monitoring and measurement, analysis of data, internal audits, nonconforming product reports, customer feedback, process performance, status of corrective/preventive actions, and recommendations for improvements. It is important that the decisions in these management reviews are made based on factual information about the best alternatives, and that decisions are documented, communicated, and reviewed.

Also, personnel need to feel secure in making decisions; you need to create a constructive environment, involving the right people and allowing opinions and information to be shared.

In any decision-making process there is some degree of uncertainty, and it is important to use risk analysis, evaluating the risks associated with the various options to ensure they are manageable.

FACTUAL APPROACH TO DECISION MAKING

Focus: Quality—Customer

1 What decisions were made in the last management review? What were the decisions based on? Is this information made available to those who need it?

2 Are decisions and actions based on factual analysis of data (generated from monitoring and measurement), and balanced with past business experience?
  a. Customer satisfaction
  b. Product requirement conformity
  c. Process and product trends and characteristics
  d. Suppliers

3 Are you confident in the tools used for business analysis for your marketing program?

4 Are you able to align revenue and sales operations, improve employee productivity, and reduce errors?

5 What follow-up is done on actions to check if data was accurate and reliable?

6 Does management provide a supportive environment for personnel to make creative decisions, or is it a "play it safe," "pass the blame" atmosphere?

7 How has the organization used technology to support faster decision making and information sharing (tracking of issues online, web meetings enabling participants to solve problems collaboratively)?

Act

FACTUAL APPROACH TO DECISION MAKING

FOCUS: QUALITY—CUSTOMER

_____

_____

_____

_____

_____

_____

_____

_____

_____

_____

_____

_____

_____

_____

_____

_____

_____

_____

_____

_____

_____

_____

Mutually Beneficial Supplier Relationship

An organization and its suppliers are interdependent and a mutually beneficial relationship enhances the ability of both to create value.

Today, businesses are very interdependent on each other, their suppliers, and their customers. Decisions should not be made in isolation, as they can have an impact on others in the marketplace and may have a detrimental effect on the organization.

Organizations depend upon their suppliers. Organizations' success is dependent on having a strong and viable supply chain and ensuring cost controls, quality, and performance improvements of purchased products and services.

Your suppliers can impact your cycle time for time to market or impact your supplier costs. You need to establish supplier relationships, review rankings of key suppliers, and determine risks to the organization tied with the supplier.

Involve key suppliers in product design where applicable so you can utilize their knowledge, expertise, and innovation. Ensure your personnel have a thorough knowledge of the supplier's processes, costs, and capabilities in order to meet current and future needs. Your suppliers can also help you understand your competition and industry trends.

You may also be able to negotiate extended terms on purchases so that you can utilize your cash flow in a different area.

Be careful not to rely on only one supplier. Many companies were caught when the tsunami hit Japan, as they were getting materials from suppliers in this area. The unavailability of one part for an automotive industry could shut down assembly lines for a long time period if other suppliers were not available. Also if other suppliers were found, the item could have an increased cost factor tied to the part that was not considered.

Perform supplier audits to ensure that management system structure meets international standards—supporting the system of working with nonconforming products and having systems in place to analyze root causes and processes to continually improve their operations, which in turn support the continual improvement of your quality management system.

Assess & Reflect #15

MUTUALLY BENEFICIAL SUPPLIER RELATIONSHIP

Focus: Quality—Customer

1. How does the organization build and manage supplier relationship? Are any of the following conducted, and if not, what is in place?
   a. Financial risk analysis of high-risk suppliers
   b. Supplier surveys
   c. Supplier audits
   d. Executive visits
   e. Approved vendors in classification categories
2. Do you conduct supplier audits on your key suppliers?
3. Who are your key suppliers? Where are they located? With increased costs tied to oil and gas, are your suppliers in areas that will be impacted by these fluctuating supply-chain costs?
4. Does your organization have a reliable forecasting of its material needs for suppliers?
5. Do you keep your suppliers informed about what is going on in your company?
   a. Employee changes
   b. New product launches
   c. Special promotions you have planned
6. How do you treat your suppliers?
   a. Payments on time
   b. Communicate openly with them
   c. Visit them regularly
   d. Invite them to your location
   e. Give them sufficient lead time to process requirements

Act

MUTUALLY BENEFICIAL SUPPLIER RELATIONSHIP

FOCUS: QUALITY—CUSTOMER

_____
_____
_____
_____
_____
_____
_____
_____
_____
_____
_____
_____
_____
_____
_____
_____
_____
_____
_____
_____
_____
_____
_____
_____
_____
_____
_____

Note

1. Principle Quotes are from the ISO 9000:2005 and ISO 9004:2009, For a complete document on the quality management principles, go to www.iso.org.

CHAPTER 7

Principles for Environmental Management Systems

C ompanies are judged by their reputations and their codes of ethics. Business management requires you as the leaders within the organization to understand the principles you have for environmental management and how you will conduct your affairs. What do you value? What value are you creating tied with environmental management for your organization, for your customers, and for the world or society?

A company's environmental management system (EMS) standardized to ISO 14001 is used to assist business managers to constantly improve their environmental commitment to prevention of pollution, identifying their environmental business risks. The organization's management system needs to be appropriate to the nature, scale, and environmental impacts of its activities, products, and services.

ISO 14001's definition of environment is "surroundings in which an organization operates, including air, water, land, natural resources, flora, fauna, humans and their interrelation. Note: Surroundings in this context extend from within an organization to the global system."

This is the environment that an organization needs to consider in its management system.

There are many benefits tied to developing an EMS, from providing a system that would provide due diligence to managing your business from reactionary to anticipatory, shifting your focus from end-of-pipe to point source control. This also can result in improved cost efficiency in operations, due to reductions in consumption for energy, water, and materials or changes in materials used in production due to environmental impacts. There may be reduced insurance contributions and claims due to environmental programs put in place, and increased sales due to environmentally green products.

Companies today recognize the importance of commitment to sustainable development, which ties closely with integration of environment and economic goals. Due to social media, consumers want to purchase a product from a company that has a long-term commitment to a cause, such as the protection of clean water, environmental climate change, health and disease, and economic development.

Many marketing initiatives today are tied to environmental events, such as Earth Day, with the recycling and reuse of e-waste and empty ink cartridges. Many companies have gotten on the bandwagon to market themselves and their products through their efforts to reduce environmental impact on the economy, from the recycling of tires (rubber), mattresses, diapers, glass, and cable (copper) to the recovery of oil spills.

Industry Leaders Improving Our World

Industry leaders will be outlined in this section to help us to understand the urgency and importance of business leaders' involvement in thinking not only of their own business but also of how it interconnects with others around the world to improve the sustainability of our world.

BASF

I was so impressed with reading an event summary done by the Toronto Sustainability Speakers Series, by Brad Zarnett, June 12, 2013, on

"Innovation at BASF: Courage to Dream of a Better World," by Carles Navarro, President.

BASF is the chemical company that produces chemicals used in industries such as agriculture, health, energy, transportation, packaging, health, etc. Navarro is an innovation person, who embraces sustainability for the good of the world. He was quoted as saying, "We make chemistry for a sustainable future." They understand the needs of the world and that our current rate of resource consumption is not sustainable.

It is estimated that by 2050 there will be 9 million people on the planet and the supply will not meet the demand. BASF's culture of innovation dates back to its roots in Germany in the nineteenth century. Its success was working internally and externally, in collaboration with private industry and academia to develop many breakthrough chemical innovations with its concept of *Verbund*, a German word meaning *linked* or *integrated* to the maximum degree. This philosophy is behind BASF's approach not only to research and innovation but also to manufacturing, infrastructure, and processes.

The article described how BASF applied these principles by using the by-products of one industrial plant as the starting materials for another. Their new tool, called SEEBALANCE, was developed to measure and analyze their products and processes according to three pillars of sustainability: ecology, economy, and society.

Being innovative, setting clear goals, and being willing to take risks are key to managing our unsustainable world, to thinking out of the box, and having the courage to try new opportunities.

Shell International Limited

Many companies have outlined their business principles, such as Shell International Limited, which first published them in 1976 and have updated them every four or five years.

Its eight business principles are: economic; competition; business integrity; political activities; health, safety, security, and the environment; local communities; communication and engagement; and compliance.

Environmental Principles

ENVIRONMENTAL MANAGEMENT SYSTEM PRINCIPLES*

- Leadership
- Focus: environment—prevention of pollution
- Continual improvement
- System approach to management
- Compliance with legal and other requirements
- Performance evaluation
- Management of resources
- Operational control
- Emergency preparedness and response

---

* ISO does not outline principles for environmental management.

Environmental Management

Principles★ are created to help companies maintain and succeed in their businesses in all markets through all circumstances.

Leadership

Top management recognizes the priority of environmental management as an integral part for its business success, social responsibility, and sustainability. It leads by establishing vision, policy, objectives, programs, and practices to ensure its commitment to the prevention of pollution and that environmental performance is integrated in the way they do business, throughout the organization.

★The following quotes on principles are from Pilot Performance Resources Management Inc.'s speaking series on "Driving Business Sustainability," helping companies maintain and succeed in their business in all markets through all circumstances.

Senior management clearly articulates the commitment to prevention of pollution and environmental performance in its vision and policy statements. Managers then formulate a plan to fulfill the policy. This starts with the identification of risks tied with environmental aspects (cause) of its activities, products, and services that it can control and have influence over that could cause an impact (effect) on the environment. It is important to identify risks not only in day-to-day processes but also prior to new projects or programs being launched and the decommissioning or closing of a site. Extending environmental influence into value-chain implications for procurement also needs to be evaluated.

The board of directors needs to be aware of the operational risks tied not only with quality but also with environment and health and safety.

Environmental performance is accomplished by identifying and reducing environmental impacts by use of processes, practices, techniques, materials, products, services, or energy, to avoid, reduce, or control the creation, emission, or discharge of any type of pollutant or waste. This can include some of the following: source reduction or elimination; process/product/service changes; efficient use of resources; and material and energy substitution, reuse, recovery, recycling, reclamation, and treatment.

In the planning stage of an environmental management system, objectives and targets need to be established by top management for strategic plans to improve and prevent environmental impacts, whether internally or externally. Managers need to understand the risks, opportunities and stakeholder expectations to set objectives. These objectives need to be supported by programs, or, as business understands them, as projects, outlining the designation of responsibility and the means and time frame needed to complete the programs. These need to be reviewed on a regular basis to ensure that completion and results meet the required objectives and strategic planning.

The organization ensures that the significant environmental aspects are considered not only when establishing and implementing its environmental management system but also when it is maintained. Controls are put in place for prevention of pollution through operational controls and adequate resources.

Communicating the importance of effective environmental management is crucial so that all employees view the management of "risks" as part of their daily responsibilities and the importance of continual improvement.

During the company's management review of its management systems (MS) top management will review its commitment to prevention of pollution, assessing continuing suitability and effectiveness of its operations for prevention of pollution, opportunities for improvement, and the need for changes to the MS.

Sustainability Leaders
GlobeScan/Sustainability Survey

Leadership is crucial in environmental management. Ahead are examples of some key sustainability leaders and what they have done in their companies for sustainability.

The area of sustainability has been a hot topic, and in 2013 a GlobeScan/Sustainability Survey was conducted in 73 countries, looking at the leaders of sustainability. This section gives a brief review of its findings and some of the key companies.

The report can be found at www.globescan.com, under "News—Reports." It was not surprising to see under the key findings that "national governments were seen as demonstrating the poorest leadership on sustainability last year." Social entrepreneurs are perceived as the leaders in advancing sustainability in all regions except Africa and the Middle East. Unilever captured the top spot for the third year in a row. The top companies listed as being perceived as leaders in sustainability in their business strategy are: Unilever, Patagonia, Interface, Wal-Mart, GE, Marks & Spencer, Puma, Nike, Coca-Cola, Natura, IBM, Google, Nestlé, and Novo Nordisk.

The report outlined the reasons Unilever was considered a sustainability leader, starting back in 2010, when the company identified evidence-based metrics for impact, as well as a focus on developing sustainable food, with ambitious goals set for the organization supported by the CEO's leadership through their Sustainability Living Plan.

It cannot be stressed enough that the setting of goals and direction for the organization is key to its leadership—not only the goals at high level but also the support throughout the organization in focusing its objectives to meet those goals by the activities that are being done.

Unilever

Paul Polman is the chief executive officer for Unilever, a Dutch man on a mission, with a commitment to sustainability and creativity in new product development to meet environmental challenges, from waterless shampoo to eco-friendly, one-rinse fabric softeners.

He has put efforts in place to be responsible for providing solutions not only for environmental initiatives but also for scaling up nutrition in the world. He is involved in initiatives put on by the World Economic Forum to help malnourished youngsters, especially the 170 million children affected by stunting, and to help Africans create sustainable food systems so they are able to produce enough food for themselves and to export. In Kenya or Tanzania, over 100,000 families depend on Unilever for their livelihoods.

In July 2013, the *Independent* newspaper in the UK did a story on Mr. Polman entitled "Chief Executive of Unilever Paul Polman Is a Boss with More on His Plate Than Sales Figures." He is not only thinking about soap and shampoo today; he hosts a summit on the problem of world hunger. It is interesting to note that the world population in 2012 was 7 billion people and it is still growing; the average person produces 4.4 pounds of waste per day, or around a ton of waste each year. The article reports that "Mr. Polman, and Nestlé's chairman, Peter Brabeck-Letmathe, has been pressing David Cameron, the Prime Minister of the United Kingdom, to end the use of biofuels made from food crops, claiming that many varieties are worse for climate change than the fossil fuels they were created to replace. He also called for a halt to illegal deforestation driven by the need for raw materials such as palm oil."

Mr. Polman understands the global marketplace and is taking his established brands from a footprint already in India and Indonesia to emerging markets, as the slower growth is in North America and Europe.

In the Bloomberg story "Unilever CEO Paul Polman on Earnings, Price Growth,"[1] Mr. Polman said that 54 percent of their business was in emerging markets, and that the company's focus was on cutting costs that consumers are not willing to pay for and not compromising research and development, or advertising. He views what is happening in the world as a unique opportunity to regain credibility for sustainability, focusing on the environment. Look to what you can influence.

Unilever's website outlines its purpose and principles to succeed, stating, "The highest standards of corporate behavior towards everyone we work with, the communities we touch and the environment on which we have an impact." It focuses on always working with integrity, positive impact, continuous commitment, setting out their aspirations, and working with others.

Corporate sustainability leaders like Unilever incorporate long-term economic, environmental, and social aspects into their business strategies, which achieve long-term shareholder value by reducing costs and risks.

Dow Jones Sustainability Index

Unilever has been the sustainability leader on the Dow Jones Sustainability Index (DJSI) for 12 straight years.

The DJSI was launched in 1999 and is the first global index tracking the financial performance of leading sustainability companies worldwide, which provides asset managers with reliable and objective benchmarking, as well as providing investors with sustainability-driven investment portfolios.

Today, shareholders demand sound financial returns, long-term economic growth, and transparent financial accounting. This then leads to a high standard of public reporting, requiring a company to have a management system structure in place to provide this type of information.

The framework or structure I recommend is to international standards that are accepted in over 190 countries. The framework for environmental standards includes the review of identification of environmental impacts and the setting of measurable objectives, which can then be audited through the internal audit process and the third-party audit process, either for registration or self-declaration, providing a verification of an environmental management system process in place.

The DJSI is offered by S&P Dow Jones Indices, the world's largest global resource for index-based concepts, data, and research, and RobecoSAM, which is the internationally recognized leading pioneer in corporate sustainability assessment (CSA) methodology.

They use the best-in-class approach for inclusion in the DJSI; therefore, companies continually intensify their sustainability initiatives, benefiting not only the corporation but also the investors, customers, and ultimately society and the environment.

The DJSI comprises global, regional (North America, Europe, South Pacific), and country benchmarks, as well as emerging markets. Table 7.1 lists super-sector leaders for 2012 in the Dow Jones Sustainability Index.[2]

TABLE 7.1

Super-Sector Leaders		
Bayerische Motoren Werke AG (BMW)	Automobiles & Parts	Germany
Australia & New Zealand Banking Group Ltd	Banks	Australia
UPM-Kymmene OYJ	Basic Resources	Finland
Akzo Nobel NV	Chemicals	Netherlands
GS Engineering & Construction Corp	Construction & Materials	South Korea
Itaúsa—Investimentos Itaú SA	Financial Services	Brazil
Unilever NV	Food & Beverage	Netherlands
Roche Holding AG	Health Care	Switzerland
Siemens AG	Industrial Goods and Services	Germany
Swiss Re	Insurance	Switzerland
Telenet Group Holding NV	Media	Belgium
Repsol SA	Oil & Gas	Spain
Koninklijke Philips Electronics NV	Personal & Household	Netherlands
GPT Group	Real Estate	Australia
Lotte Shopping Co. Ltd.	Retail	South Korea
Alcatel-Lucent SA	Technology	France
KT Corp.	Telecommunications	South Korea
Air France-KLM	Travel & Leisure	France
Iberdrola SA	Utilities	Spain

Coca-Cola

Muhtar A. Kent, a Turkish-American business executive, is the chairman and chief executive officer of the Coca-Cola Company. Coca-Cola is one of the top-ten chosen companies for sustainability. He believes being a resilient company in 2013 requires being focused on what matters most, shedding what is wasteful and unproductive, and communicating with customers and stakeholders.

It has developed innovations that are focused on reducing packaging, energy, and water footprints, and improving the well-being of communities it serves. Coca-Cola has conducted 386 community water projects in 94 countries, working with local government and partners, such as World Wildlife Fund, US Agency for International Development, the Nature Conservancy, and CARE, building resilience through its water stewardship efforts.

It has partnered with Dean Kamen of DEKA R&D, bringing their Slingshot water purification technology to communities where potable water access is limited in schools and centers in Africa and Latin America.

It plans to expand and deliver a full-service community center with electricity, Internet access, and vaccination storage, as it sees this as an investment in the future prosperity and progress of the communities in which they operate.

Patagonia

Patagonia, a 35-year-old company, grew from making tools for climbers into a clothing manufacturer not only for climbing but also for skiing, snowboarding, surfing, fishing, etc. Since the 1980s, it has donated time, services, and at least 1 percent of sales to hundreds of grassroots environmental groups all over the world, who work to help reverse the tide.

It has taken unbelievable steps in being responsible by providing $38 million dollars over the years. Its philosophy is that it is taking ownership for nonrenewable resources by taxing themselves 1 percent on sales, not profits. There are over 1,200 organizations that are a part of this grow-ing initiative; those funds go to over 3,429 organizations worldwide.[3]

It contributes its success to being transparent—open and honest—about its footprint to all stakeholders. It openly discusses success and challenges and has made sustainability a part of its business before it became trendy—a true commitment.

Interface

Interface's president, Ray Anderson, is a true business leader at his or-ganization and in the world. He stated in a TED program that theft is a crime and what we are stealing is our children's future. His company has revolutionized the carpet industry and plans to have zero environ-mental footprint by 2020. He stated that we live in a web of life and we have a choice to make while we are here on earth—to either hurt it or help it. What will you do?

All organizations today need to take a part in helping to sustain our world. Governments have the biggest control, managing our water, our energy, and our waste. Many governments today are going to pri-vate partnerships for management of these areas. Will this ensure proper management of these areas? I am not totally convinced; it will depend on the requirements to improve on environmental impacts.

Having an environmental management system that meets the ISO 14001 criteria will ensure that an organization has identified its envi-ronmental risks or impacts and has put a framework for managing its business in place, setting strategic plans not only for improving cost measures tied to consumption of energy and materials, reductions in waste and scrap, and reformulation of products to conserve resources and many other initiatives, but also for managing its business operations effectively and efficiently.

Companies that show stakeholders that they are truly doing some-thing to save our planet are those that people want to work for, and therefore they will attract the best people in the future. Due to loss of managers from the grey tsunami, there will be limited choices.

LEADERSHIP

FOCUS: ENVIRONMENT—PREVENTION OF POLLUTION

❶ Has your organization made a commitment to prevention of pollution and improvement of environmental performance?
   a. How has your organization improved the environmental impact on the world?
   b. Is your company a catalyst for change in the environment? How?

❷ Why is environmental management important to your organization? Do you presently have environmental concepts in your business practice, but not an environmental management system?

❸ Is your business sustainable? Would environmental management help to improve your costs? Help you to have a competitive edge? Would you be willing to try?

❹ Is your company innovative in managing the following? What have you done? What are the risks if you do not address these areas?
   a. Energy
   b. Water consumption
   c. Waste recycling
   d. Waste reuse
   e. Material substitution

❺ Commitments to environmental management are tied to your budget. What commitments and innovation has your organization made to improving environmental management? Are they measureable?
   a. Within your organization's activities and services—reducing your environmental footprint
   b. Designing and manufacturing innovative products that reduce environmental and social impacts
   c. Outside—providing funding to environmental groups (e.g., 1 percent for the planet)

❻ Has your organization reduced environmental impacts associated with following?
   a. Natural resources (consumption of energy, water)
   b. Reduction of solid waste generation

    c. Air pollution—greenhouse gases

    d. Wastewater effluent

    e. Soil or land contamination

    f. Noise

    g. Smell

7 Have you improved your environmental impacts? How?

8 Do you manage your environmental business risks more effectively than your competitors? Do your business competitors have an EMS in place or are they in the process?

9 Does your organization have a sustainability program in place? Do you report on sustainability?

10 How can your company do more with less?

11 How do you prepare for growth in an era of natural resource scarcity?

12 How do you ensure that your environmental commitments are taken into account when maintaining your environmental management system?

13 What have you done in the following areas for prevention of pollution?

    a. Production: Changes in equipment or processes to reduce emissions or consumption of resources

    b. Purchasing: Changes in types of materials ordered

    c. Maintenance: Changes in chemicals used; changes in energy-saving lightbulbs

    d. Life cycle: Disposal of products

14 What do you benchmark your success in environmental sustainability to?

    a. Reduction of risk

    b. Increased value

15 How does your organization review the risks tied with its processes, projects, changes, and business shut-downs or closings?

16 How do you inform the consumer about the safe use, storage, and disposal of your products?

17 How is the environment impacting your business?

18 How has your organization lead in environmental in emerging countries?

LEADERSHIP

Focus: Environment—Prevention of Pollution

_____

_____

_____

_____

_____

_____

_____

_____

_____

_____

_____

_____

_____

_____

_____

_____

_____

_____

_____

_____

_____

_____

_____

_____

_____

Continual Improvement—Prevention of Pollution

Senior management's main tasks in leadership are to forecast and assess challenges and opportunities for ongoing continual improvement in overall environmental performance.

Continual improvement is a journey, an ongoing commitment by top management, requiring employee engagement and stakeholder support, and needs to be applied internationally or wherever the company is conducting business. Top management's vision is outlined in its strategy, policies, and contingency plans for continual improvement, and at the same time focuses on long-term profitability.

The company may see breakthrough improvements in energy conservation tied with reduction in costs or incremental improvements over time in how one manages waste.

Unlike quality management, which deals with continual improvement of the product at the beginning of design and/or operational control, environmental management deals with the consequences of its activities, products, and services for continual improvement and the input of new and changing technology and legal and consumer requirements.

In order to achieve improvements in environmental performance consistent with the organization's policy statement, the management system needs to be communicated and supported by its stakeholders, as well as reviewed for continual improvement.

Areas within the management system structure that deal with this commitment are many, from the planning stage of setting and reviewing its measurable objectives, targets, and programs, to its implementation stage of defining roles and responsibilities and training personnel, to its improvement stage. The monitoring and measurement of performance, operational controls, and conformity with environmental objectives and targets to continual improvement is verified through the company's internal audits, corrective/preventive action system and management reviews.

The board of directors should be provided with copies of internal and third-party audits to understand the status of the company's operations.

Internal audits are subject to different initiatives, whether they are international management system requirements, risks, or compliance to legal requirements (e.g., environmental regulations or Sarbanes-Oxley, known as Public Company Accounting Reform and Investor Protection Act [SOX]). In order for an audit to be effective, the internal audit process needs to be conducted by independent, competent staff. If an individual works for an organization, he or she might not be objective in exercising professional judgment. Top management and in some cases investors rely on this audit process and, therefore, the need for third-party audits.

Assess & Reflect #17

CONTINUAL IMPROVEMENT

Focus: Environment—Prevention of Pollution

① What activities at your organization impact the environment?
   a. Positively
   b. Negatively
② How does top management encourage innovation in environmental management?
③ Increases in rates for consumption and materials will continue to rise, so can your organization afford not to introduce environmental programs that would reduce usage and costs?
④ What measurements indicate the improvement of your EMS?
   a. Increased employee engagement
   b. Reduced costs in facility management—energy, waste
   c. Reduced costs in production
   d. Increased productivity
   e. Reduced material costs
   f. Reduced logistics costs
   g. Increased revenue through branding—tied with environment
   h. Other
⑤ Is your management system designed to ensure ongoing continual improvement? How?
   a. Who are your change agents or leaders?
   b. Do you have a change management process in place?
   c. What other opportunities do you see to improve the success of your business?
⑥ Is the commitment to continual improvement visible throughout the organization? Visible to your customers? Is it supported with resources? Is there a plan of action? Is it encouraged? Rewarded?
⑦ Has your EMS been able to create new business opportunities or influence new capital investments?
⑧ Has your environmental program(s) helped improve your company's image?
⑨ What has changed in your organization's performance due to continual improvement?

(continued)

Asses & Reflect (continued)

⑩ How does your organization deal with ineffective results?

⑪ Does your company contribute to research tied with the environmental impact of its products, processes, and wastes to minimize adverse impacts? What areas?

⑫ How will newly defined objectives support the company's guiding principles?

⑬ What have you learned about the effectiveness and efficiency of your management system from your internal and third-party audit process?

⑭ Are you able to manage risk more effectively?

⑮ Has your organization improved in prevention of pollution? What opportunities for improvement (OFIs) are identified now and for the future?

Act

CONTINUAL IMPROVEMENT

Focus: Prevention of Pollution

System Approach to Management

A system approach is identifying, understanding, and managing integrated and interdependent processes and their risks that contribute to the organization's environmental management system effectiveness.

Reviewing the inputs and outputs of each process as only a section of the company as a whole contributes to understanding the effects on other processes within the organization. This approach helps managers avoid analyzing problems in isolation.

The most common system model used for environmental management is the ISO 14001. There have been other models, such as the European Eco-Management and Audit Scheme (EMAS) and the Responsible Care model, developed by the American Chemical Council (ACC).

Many organizations, when implementing their environmental management system (EMS) to ISO 14001 requirements, have used the PDCA methodology, based on Deming's "Plan-Do-Check-Act," implemented in post-WWII Japan.

The focus in the twenty-first century has been on the environmental revolution, and the ISO management system's emphasis has been on continual improvement. In 1995, I developed the Three-Step Process: Identify, Insure, Improve™ for management system implementation. These three steps can be applied not only to quality but also to implementation of an environmental management system (see Figure 7.1).

FIGURE 7.1

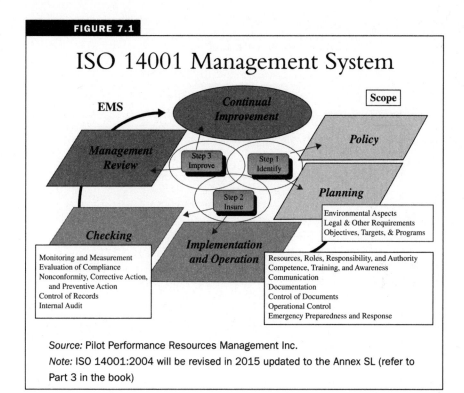

ISO 14001 Management System

Source: Pilot Performance Resources Management Inc.

Note: ISO 14001:2004 will be revised in 2015 updated to the Annex SL (refer to Part 3 in the book)

SYSTEM APPROACH TO MANAGEMENT

Focus: Environment—Prevention of Pollution

1. Do you view the environmental management system (EMS) meeting ISO 14001 as an advantage for you in improving your organization's business sustainability? How?

2. Has the company adopted the ISO 14001 standard as its business management system for managing its environmental issues?

3. Does top management understand the requirements of the standard? How has this been confirmed?

4. Does top management understand the benefits of a system approach following international standards?

5. Do you have a separate management system structure to manage environmental issues or have you integrated environmental issues into your business management system framework?
   a. Integrated with occupational health and safety
   b. Integrated with quality, environment, health and safety

6. What opportunities does the EMS create for the company?

7. What low-hanging fruit has your company worked on for environmental improvement?

8. To understand your system approach has your company done process mapping?

9. Did you engage your internal/external stakeholders in the identification of environmental risks and programs tied with your process?

10. Is your system approach transparent to your engaged stakeholders?

11. Do you integrate your environmental management with your quality and health and safety? Why? Why not?

12. Do you have an integrated management system in place now? If not, do you think an integrated management system will remove duplication of activities and documents?

Act

SYSTEM APPROACH TO MANAGEMENT

FOCUS: PREVENTION OF POLLUTION

_____
_____
_____
_____
_____
_____
_____
_____
_____
_____
_____
_____
_____
_____
_____
_____
_____
_____
_____
_____
_____
_____
_____
_____

Compliance with Legal and Other Requirements

A commitment to comply with applicable legal and other requirements to which the organization subscribes related to its environmental aspects and impacts is a permanent objective of the organization.

Top management makes a commitment to comply with legal and other associated requirements. The organization needs to determine the applicable legal requirements related to its environmental aspects, which are the activities, products, or services that interact with the environment.

When identifying legal requirements, look at where and how you get information tied to legal to ensure that you keep updated and can understand the regulations binding your organization.

The organization is also committed to identify other requirements, which could be meeting your industry's codes of practice, such as Responsible Care in the chemical industry, collective agreements, leasing requirements, corporate head office requirements, best practices, and permit requirements.

The list of applicable environmental legal requirements for your organization needs to include the applicable tasks required to maintain compliance.

Do you need to keep records of operational controls, such as temperature readings, reports to government on volumes of pollutant releases, complete forms for tracking wastes, or apply for permits? Keeping track of environmental regulations is a full-time job. Many organizations have staff managing just this area, or they hire an outside contractor that does a compliance audit.

In some countries, a business that impacts the environment (e.g., releases contaminants into the air, land, or water; stores, transports, or disposes of waste) needs an approval from the government body to operate legally within its jurisdiction.

Generally, facilities report noncompliance to a government body, or they might have been identified through government inspections. The range of enforcement may include suspension of or amendments to approvals or issuing of orders, tickets, or fines, as in the case of the United States Environmental Protection Agency (EPA).[4]

It is interesting to note that the greatest area of enforcement is tied with hazardous waste, then contaminated water, and then soil. The judicial penalties assessed were $104,390,628.

The Office of the Auditor General of Canada's Report of the Commissioner of the Environment and Sustainable Development reported in 2011, as part of "enforcing the Canadian Environmental Protection Act, 1999, Chapter 3, that: 606 written warnings were given, 42 environmental protection compliance orders and 2 prosecutions."[5]

Assess & Reflect #19

COMPLIANCE WITH LEGAL AND OTHER REQUIREMENTS

FOCUS: ENVIRONMENT—PREVENTION OF POLLUTION

1. Has your organization identified its applicable legal and other requirements and the tasks tied to these requirements?
2. Who at your organization is responsible for overall legal and other requirements and who is responsible and accountable for the specific tasks to meet these requirements?
3. How do you keep track of changes to legislation?
4. Where are legal documents stored, such as permits and government reports? Where are paper documents filed? Are these documents scanned into the computer for access?
5. How does your organization keep track of reporting to government on environmental requirements, such as waste volumes, hazardous materials inventory, emission requirements, etc.?
6. Does your organization do a compliance audit internally or externally? How often? Yearly?
7. When your compliance audit report is received and there are noncompliance issues, how is this information processed through your management system to ensure that details on completion of action items are addressed?
8. What outstanding compliance issues does your organization have? Who is managing these and how are they documented and tracked for completion?
9. Communication of legal requirements is important for stakeholders to understand—how are these delivered at your organization?
10. Has the company received any fines, court orders, or notices of violations related to environmental issues? What cost was this to the organization? Are they:
    a. Recorded?
    b. Tracked? (non-conformity—corrective action system)
    c. Is there an improvement plan?

COMPLIANCE WITH LEGAL AND OTHER

FOCUS: PREVENTION OF POLLUTION

_____

_____

_____

_____

_____

_____

_____

_____

_____

_____

_____

_____

_____

_____

_____

_____

_____

_____

_____

_____

_____

_____

_____

Performance Evaluation

Monitoring and measurement of environmental risks, plans, practices, and performance indicators forms the basis for continual improvement. External unattached assessment, as well as internal, will identify business improvement opportunities and shortcomings and provide unbiased intelligence. Effective decisions are based on the analysis of data and information.

To survive in this global marketplace, an organization needs to determine the factors that are critical to its company's success. Being environmentally conscious or working in the green economy is at the forefront of the minds of employees, the public, the government, and your stockholders.

Many governments, as well as companies, are committed to sustainable development, having a vision of stimulating economic growth and protecting our environment without having a negative impact on future generations. Emphasis is being put on procurement, leading by example and embedding sustainable development into policy with transparent management.

Your operations or products can affect the environment in a positive or negative way. The past several of years, the focus has been on climate change and energy conservation.

The process in the management system that focuses on the measurement of business success is defining one's objectives. In order for objectives to be managed, look at the process or system your organization is using for tracking them throughout the organization. Many companies have people busy working on projects and assignments, and when asked where this information is recorded, it is outlined in many areas in the company, from project management software to Six Sigma programs, or made-up matrix documents.

For top management to lead the company, it is important that the management team is focused on working on the most important projects, as defined by the needs and expectations of not only customers but also legal and corporate requirements. It is important to remember that people within your organization know where problems exist and will observe whether resources are applied to them.

Are you doing the right things at the right time? Companies have a life cycle, and it is important to know the stage you are in. In the beginning of the book we spoke about the grey tsunami and the fact that many managers today are leaving companies for retirement in the next five years. Have you set one of your goals to ensure that the knowledge bank is captured before your managers leave your employment? Do you have an exit strategy for these managers?

In order to know if your objectives (what you want to achieve and why) support your goals (big picture) or intentions for success, you need to have measurables (key performance indicators). The objective needs to outline what you want to do, how it is to be quantified, and what the completion date for the objective will be. Following the SMART methodology, objectives need to be Specific, Measurable, Actionable, Realistic, and Timed. We all know the phrase "What gets measured, gets done."

Once objectives have been outlined and are in a tracking system, you develop a strategy or strategies for how you will meet them. Details or execution steps outline how to meet your strategy, who will be responsible, and timelines.

Return on investment (ROI) may not always be the measurement of success; it may be your own metrics showing that you have made progress toward the objectives that support your goal to improve value in the area of environmental management.

Assess & Reflect #20

PERFORMANCE EVALUATION

Focus: Environment—Prevention of Pollution

1. Are objectives and targets (projects) ongoing throughout the year and at different levels throughout the organization, supporting the organization's principles and goals?
2. What areas are your objectives and targets focused on?
3. Did the organization, when establishing and reviewing its objectives, consider:
   a. Its significant environmental aspects and impacts? Environmental risks?
   b. Legal and other requirements? Compliance?
   c. Technological options?
   d. Its financial, operational, and business requirements?
   e. Views of interested parties?
   f. Targets and programs to implement to achieve goals?
4. What methodology does your organization use for setting objectives (Six Sigma, Lean)? Do you look at alternatives before selecting action programs or projects?
5. What objectives and targets in your business would you feel proud of today?
6. What measurement have you used with your key objectives for the last quarter? This measurement should tell you whether you have completed the objective successfully.
7. What system(s) do you have in place to track or monitor the objectives at different levels within your organization?
8. Has your company capitalized on the funding available for improving heating and air conditioning or lighting retrofits?
9. What systems do you have in place to measure your successes or failures?
   a. Nonconformance system—identify what they are—tracking how they are managed
   b. Corrective action system
   c. Preventive action system
   d. Inspections
   e. Audit types: internal, third party, supplier
   f. Best management practices
   g. Other:

Act

PERFORMANCE EVALUATION

FOCUS: MONITORING AND MEASUREMENT OF PREVENTION OF POLLUTION

_____

_____

_____

_____

_____

_____

_____

_____

_____

_____

_____

_____

_____

_____

_____

_____

_____

_____

_____

_____

_____

_____

_____

_____

_____

_____

_____

Management of Resources

Top management ensures adequate and effective management of our resources: land (natural resources), labor (human resources), and capital (financial resources).

Management ensures the availability and investment of resources that will establish, implement, maintain, and improve its environmental management system. These resources include not only human resources with specialized skills and competence-ensuring capabilities but also infrastructure, materials, financial resources, and technology.

Support is also required in implementing the environmental management system, which is done through operation control, EMS documentation, communication, and emergency preparedness. The use of information technology (IT) to manage real-time activities and the management of resources improves productivity and profitability.

When determining the resource needs, a CEO looks to the processes and activities required to meet strategic plans and strategies aligned with the objectives and performance targets. These targets may change, based on customer or corporate demands.

Activities ask for and compete for the resources at hand, and needs may change as work progresses. Transparency is crucial in managing business to peak performance. Criteria for investment of resources include sustainability considerations, including economic, social, and environmental, and the evaluation of investment risks.

An organization needs to focus on the "triple bottom line," which I refer to as the three Ps: Performance, Productivity, and Profits (economic), which engage people (social) for the planet (environmental).

Roles need to be defined so that the organization is clear about its applicable responsibilities in order to facilitate effective environmental management. An organization has a responsibility to many groups, from its shareholders, protecting their investments; to their customers, ensuring the provision of products and services that offer value in terms of quality, price, safety, and environmental impact. It also has a responsibility to its employees, providing them with safe work environments and an opportunity for their involvement and commitment in initiatives, as well as rewarding them for their innovations and improvements.

To be successful you also need to develop mutually beneficial relationships and partnerships with others, such as contractors and value-chain suppliers, who support your principles and environmental requirements for life-cycle thinking (design and development, purchasing). Another key group that an organization has responsibilities to is to society, to conduct its business according to applicable laws and regulations and for its security, health and safety, and the environment.

In an environmental management system structure, top management appoints a specific management representative(s) who, irrespective of his or her responsibilities, will also ensure that an EMS is established, implemented, and maintained to the international standard and reports to top management on the performance and recommended improvements for the EMS. Therefore, it is imperative to keep the management representative(s) fully informed on matters affecting conditions of the management system structure and include him or her in decisions affecting the management system itself.

Identify performance expectations tied to the organization's goals and objectives. Work to ensure that personnel can fully develop and utilize their capabilities, providing recognition of performance for improving performance, productivity, and profitability.

For most personnel, new efficiency initiatives mean "change" and more work, and in some cases the change brings about a feeling of uncertainty. Top management can help personnel be accountable through performance management, by creating a work environment that promotes communication, participation, innovation, feedback, and cooperation through engagement, and by empowering personnel to participate in decisions affecting the organization's effectiveness and efficiency by being involved from the start of the initiatives and seeing them through to their achievement. A strong change management process is critical.

Being able to interface with the organization's planning, budgeting, finance, and resource management requirements by keeping abreast of current technology can improve the effectiveness and efficiency of the management system. Many software programs exist today that help management make fast-paced business decisions that can positively affect the growth of its company, while monitoring the performance requirements set out by the organization.

Identifying responsibilities is the first step tied to human resource management, and then the organization shall ensure that people performing tasks for it that have the potential of causing a significant environmental impact are competent on the basis of education, training, or experience. Associated records need to be retained that provide the due diligence.

Persons working for an organization or on its behalf (contractors) need to understand the importance of conformity with the company's policy and procedures. It is important for the individuals to understand the environmental aspects and impacts associated with their work and the requirements for emergency preparedness. Today with many of the workers coming from many different countries, the challenge is to have documents for training in a form (pictures) that they will understand.

While doing an audit on a company that had over 500 employees, I had reviewed excellent production documents that had been written in English and were posted on boards close to the relevant work area; however, when I spoke to the individuals about their tasks on the floor, I found that these people could not read the information, as they did not read English.

In another audit I was involved with, a gentleman was responsible for the handling and disposal of chemicals for the company. He could not read English and was not aware of the environment, health, and safety information on the labels or its material safety data sheets; therefore the person did not understand the hazards and proper disposal guidelines tied to hazardous chemicals.

With new technology in training we have the opportunity to have videos developed economically that provide information about how to accomplish tasks. The old trend of long-written procedures is being replaced by visuals, outlining step-by-step tasks to complete. A company needs to ensure the competencies of those responsible for areas that can have an impact on not only the environment but also the health and safety of those involved.

Key resources besides our human resources are our natural resources. Many organizations have looked at the design of their products or services and evaluated the materials they are utilizing. In the beginning of the section on environmental principles I outlined what Unilever's CEO, Mr. Polman, and Nestlé's chairman, Mr. Brabeck-Letmathe, have been working on with the prime minister in the UK to end the use of biofuels made from food crops.

Is there something in your industry that you can challenge to make a change that would benefit the use and consumption of our natural resources?

Assess & Reflect #21

MANAGEMENT OF RESOURCES

Focus: Environment—Prevention of Pollution

❶ What financial commitments have been made to the area of environmental improvements?

❷ How are resource management allocations tracked and monitored?

❸ Has top management allocated the resources needed to meet its environmental obligations? Is it sufficient?

❹ Do the products or services you provide impact the environment?

   a. Are products you provide efficient in consumption of energy, water, and materials?

   b. Can products be reused, recycled, and disposed of safely?

❺ What resources do you require for your product development and do any of these impact the environment?

   a. Can you change to another material?

   b. Who are your suppliers for the materials? Do you have backup suppliers?

   c. Is logistics improved with sourcing a new material?

❻ Is there something in your industry that you can challenge to make a change that would benefit the use and consumption of our natural resources? What is it?

❼ Does your organization have a vice president who is accountable for reporting progress on environmental matters to the board?

❽ Who is the environmental management system (EMS) representative or coordinator?

   a. Is the person a senior manager with sufficient authority, competence, and resources?

   b. Is the appointed person knowledgeable and responsible?

   c. Has he or she reported to top management on the performance of the EMS? When was the last report by the EMS representative to top management? Were there areas of improvement that came out of the review?

d. Does the representative ensure that workers and contractors are aware of the environmental issues and update them on legal requirements or changes tied to the environmental program?

e. Does the EMS representative work using a team approach with top management to relay information so that department unit managers are responsible for their own areas?

9 How do you ensure that personnel are competent in the areas in which they work?

10 What areas have been identified for improving environmental issues in the area of training?

11 What type of documented procedures do you have in place for environmental management? Do they include pictures?

Act

MANAGEMENT OF RESOURCES

FOCUS: ENVIRONMENT—PREVENTION OF POLLUTION

_____

_____

_____

_____

_____

_____

_____

_____

_____

_____

_____

_____

_____

_____

_____

_____

_____

_____

_____

_____

_____

_____

_____

_____

_____

Operational Control

Establish, implement, monitor, measure, and maintain with change management control of functions, activities, and processes that can impact the environment.

Top management leads by ensuring that process activities that were identified as having significant environmental impacts or legal requirements put operational controls in place. Operational controls may be in the form of operating procedures, preventative maintenance, equipment controls, etc. that contribute to the prevention of pollution.

Consideration needs to be given not only to normal operations but also to abnormal and emergency situations, as well as ongoing improvements or projects. For example, when controlling air emissions from a manufacturing process you need process controls and procedures for operational control of the equipment, emergency plans, and standing operating procedures; when there is a shutdown of the equipment, there may be other operating controls that are required.

Facilities need to be designed and managed, taking into consideration the property in which they are situated and the surrounding areas: whether they are residential or industrial and the impact they have on the air, water, land, flora, and fauna. Operational procedures should also address suitable maintenance of equipment and continuing process capability and regulatory compliance. A preventative maintenance program could save time and money, materials, chemicals, energy, etc. if areas are routinely managed.

The environmental standard for ISO 14001 requires that operations related to identified significant environmental aspects, which are carried out in an initial environmental review when setting up an environmental management system, establish documented procedures to control situations where their absence could lead to deviations, stipulating the operating criteria. Documents assist in ensuring that internal controls are complete, properly approved, and maintained, and revised when changes occur.

The following are examples of operational control procedures that your organization may have in place: production/manufacturing, procurement, logistics, energy management, waste management, materials management (including capital asset disposal), chemical management, wastewater treatment, operation and maintenance of equipment (boilers, fume hoods, storage tanks/silos), real estate acquisition or construction (demolition, salvage), contractor orientation, facility management (snow and ice removal, pesticides), quality assurance, laboratory operations (calibration, sampling, cleaning), emergency preparedness, start-up and shut-down of equipment, facilities, or processes, research development, construction, and decommissioning of equipment and facilities.

It is important to have other documents that are utilized by the company tied with operations referenced to the appropriate procedures, such as the site plan for the facility, process flow diagrams, listing and location of sampling points, and manufacturer's operating manuals provided for specific equipment.

In some cases, you may need to work with suppliers or contractors, who may assist you in operational controls. It is essential that you work in close partnership with them to ensure that they maintain your EMS standards in such areas as disposal of waste materials, handling and disposal of hazardous materials, and conserving of energy and water resources. It is also important to ensure that they have the correct permits and are following the associated legal requirements.

As mentioned earlier, tied with the quality management, many managers today are close to retirement and if procedures or information about business operations are not captured on paper, they may be lost forever.

It is important when developing operational control procedures that the action items are simple and concise (short form if possible), outlining the sequence of the steps and the persons involved. Should specific forms or records be required, identify what they are and where they are kept. Generally, the workers responsible for the significant aspects under consideration will be responsible for implementing the controls, and it is important that they understand what is required; this can be accomplished through on-the-job training or specific classroom training.

Today there are many automated systems at work stations outlining the operational procedures for tasks.

It is important to have a process in place for management of change, as this triggers not only changes to documents but also the need to provide training to ensure competency of relevant personnel to perform activities in conformance with the new operational controls. It is also important to communicate with appropriate contractors or suppliers related to applicable changes, as the organization is responsible for environmental impacts caused by them on their property. It is crucial then to ensure that contractors and suppliers are aware of your EMS requirements and abide by them.

Another area of concern tied to operation controls is when temporary or seasonal workers are hired to perform work within the organization. Many times young students are brought in for short periods of time, and the period of training and document review is then shortened. They can be a risk to the organization if they are not aware of your environmental impacts and how they are to conduct themselves.

OPERATIONAL CONTROL

Focus: Environment—Prevention of Pollution

❶ What activities within your organization can cause environmental impacts and has your organization implemented operational procedures for these areas?
   a. How do employees, temporary employees and contractors access them?
   b. How do you monitor that these operational controls are being followed?
   c. What nonconformances are tied with operational control at your facility?

❷ How do you ensure that appropriate workers and contractors are aware of your operational procedures?
   a. Orientation programs
   b. Contractor programs
   c. Visitor programs

❸ Facility management is an important area to ensure environmental impacts are managed. Who is responsible for this at your organization? What programs are in place to track energy and water consumption?

❹ When developing operational procedures, who is responsible for writing the procedures and who is responsible for approval of the procedures? How often are procedures reviewed and by whom?

❺ How do you manage changes that occur within your organization and ensure that these are updated in the operational procedures?

❻ How do you encourage your suppliers to improve their environmental performance and support your initiatives?
   a. Do you encourage your suppliers to have an EMS that meets ISO 14001?
   b. Do you ask your supplier for copies of its operational procedures related to the work it is providing? Or copies of permits and certificates?
   c. How do you ensure that your suppliers are meeting legal requirements tied to the environment?

    d. Do you use supply-chain software (e.g., for electronic document exchange, such as purchase orders, sharing of information on invoices, tracking inventory, determining when products are to be delivered)?

7 What operational programs do you have in place for the following?

    a. Facilities

    b. Preventative maintenance

    c. Contractors

    d. Production processes. Design reviews (environmental)

    e. Equipment performance and emissions monitoring

8 Do your procedures define who has the authority and responsibility for activities, and when, how, and with what resources they are to be performed?

Act

OPERATIONAL CONTROL

FOCUS: ENVIRONMENT—PREVENTION OF POLLUTION

_____

_____

_____

_____

_____

_____

_____

_____

_____

_____

_____

_____

_____

_____

_____

_____

_____

_____

_____

_____

_____

_____

_____

_____

_____

_____

Emergency Preparedness

The organization is responsible to ensure that it is prepared for and can respond to emergency situations and accidents and prevent or mitigate associated adverse environmental impacts.

Having an environmental management system in place ensures that the organization has made a commitment to determine risks tied to potential emergency situations and accidents that could have an impact on the environment and how it will respond to them.

An important principle for managing a business is protecting not only your work environment from possible financial implications but also persons working under the control of the organization, saving lives, protecting the community around it, and preventing casualties and disasters.

By reviewing your operations related to emergency planning you can identify areas of concern that can be rectified, such as resource requirements (equipment, supplies) and requirements not only for training personnel but also for communicating to visitors and contractors what to do in an emergency situation.

Emergency management is the process of preparing for, mitigating, responding to, and recovering from an emergency. It is a dynamic process, involving planning, reviewing legal requirements, training, conducting drills, testing equipment, and coordinating activities within the community.

Your plan needs to include a review of all possible emergencies or worst-case scenarios, such as personal injury, environmental and property damage, and product and production loss emergencies. Identification of emergency situations must be an ongoing process, especially if the facility has frequent changes in materials, equipment processes, and personnel (e.g., contract workers), and required documentation must be updated, especially after the occurrence of accidents or emergency situations.

The plan will include procedures that specify personnel responsible for managing different scenarios, resource requirements, and training, from handling fires and spills to evacuation plans. Documentation needs to be posted and communicated, outlining such things as emergency phone numbers, floor plans, drawings of service conduits (gas, water), and chemical storage areas, so correct information is available to personnel.

To assist response personnel in determining and performing effective, efficient, and coordinated emergency services and responsible remedial actions quickly, reducing recovery times and costs, you need to test your plans either through mock or simulation exercises, fire drills, or training exercises.

Contact with external resources, such as utility departments, fire departments, medical services, government, neighbors, transportation, security firms, and insurance agents can assist in understanding partnerships supporting the handling of emergency situations.

There are four main interdependent components to emergency management:

1. Prevention and mitigation—to eliminate or reduce the risks
2. Preparedness—being ready to respond to an emergency prior to an event
3. Response—act during or immediately before or after a disaster to manage its consequences
4. Recovery—to repair or restore conditions to an acceptable level after the event

Assess & Reflect #23

EMERGENCY PREPAREDNESS

FOCUS: ENVIRONMENT—PREVENTION OF POLLUTION

❶ Do you think your organization is well prepared for emergency situations? Why or why not?

❷ What types of emergencies are applicable to your organization?

❸ How do you test your emergency plans at your organization?
   a. What were your evacuation time scores?
   b. Were the results from simulation exercises recorded?

❹ What changes have you made to your emergency preparedness plan by doing tests?
   a. Changes in communication
   b. Review of traffic flow
   c. Improved training for contractors
   d. Improved training for security guards
   e. Signage enhancement
   f. Addition of other emergencies—terrorism, bullying

❺ Does your emergency preparedness plan review input from your insurance reviews?

❻ When you hire outside contractors as security, do they go through training on your emergency preparedness?

❼ If there is a gatehouse managed by outside contractors, do they know who to contact in the event of an emergency, or what to do in the event of an emergency?

❽ What emergencies could be caused by your neighbours? Do you know what risks they pose? Who to contact? Have you informed them of the risks tied with your organization?

Act

EMERGENCY PREPAREDNESS

FOCUS: ENVIRONMENT—PREVENTION OF POLLUTION

_____

_____

_____

_____

_____

_____

_____

_____

_____

_____

_____

_____

_____

_____

_____

_____

_____

_____

_____

_____

_____

_____

_____

_____

_____

_____

_____

_____

_____

Notes

1. Bloomberg TV. "Unilever CEO Paul Polman on Earnings, Price Growth." Available at www.bloomberg.com/video/73511300-unilever-ceo-paul-polman-on-earnings-price-growth.html.
2. Detailed reports can be viewed at www.sustainability-indices.com.
3. To join go to www.onepercentfortheplanet.org
4. To review the impact of compliance and enforcement activities you may wish to review the United States Environmental Protection Agency end-of-year data and trends at www.epa.gov/compliance/resources/reports/endofyear/eoy2011/eoy-data.html.
5. For copies of the report of the Commissioner of the Environment and Sustainable Development write the Office of the Auditor General of Canada, 240 Sparks Street, Stop 1047D, Ottawa, Ontario, K1A 0G6. Telephone: 613-952-0213, ext. 5000, or 1-888-761-5953 or www.oag-bvg.gc.ca/internet/docs/parl_cesd_201112_03_e.pdf.

CHAPTER 8

Principles for Occupational Health and Safety Management Systems

All business employers, from the chief executive officers through to first-level supervisors, are responsible for providing a safe and healthy workplace.

This is undertaken by identifying, assessing, and controlling the hazards in the workplace, thus reducing, eliminating, or minimizing the potential for injury, ill health, or loss of life. Whether it is failure to protect your workers against slipping or falling, chemical and gas exposure, electrocution, transportation accidents, ergonomic injuries, communicable diseases (flu, colds), hearing loss, or workplace violence, these hazards can disrupt work and may pose a serious threat to workers, resulting in lost time or loss of life.

The United States Department of Labor outlines the 10 most frequently cited standards following inspections of worksites.[1] In 2012 the following were cited: fall protection, construction; hazard communication;

scaffolding; respiratory protection; control of hazardous energy (lockout/tagout); powered industrial trucks; electrical, wiring methods, components, and equipment; ladders, construction; machines-general requirements and machine guarding; electrical systems design, general requirements. Have your supervisor review these areas in your company to address them before OSHA shows up.

Health and Safety Executive Statistics[2] for 2011 to 2012 for Britain showed a rate of fatal injury of 0.6 for every 100,000 workers. The main industrial sectors for fatal injuries were construction, agriculture, and waste and recycling. The statistics show that thousands of workers die each year from past work-related diseases and about 4,500 cancer deaths each year were due to past exposure to asbestos. The Health and Safety Executive reported new estimates to show the total cost associated with workplace injuries and ill health in Great Britain to be some £13.8 billion in 2011 prices and **27 million** working days were lost due to work-related illness and workplace injury.

In Canada, it was reported by Employment and Social Development Canada that one in every 68 employed workers in 2010 was injured and harmed on the job and received workers' compensation as a result.[3] The highest rate of injury was in construction, with a rate of injury at 24.5 cases per 1,000 employees, and then manufacturing at 24, fishing and transport, and storage and communications at 20.5.

The U.S. Bureau of Labor Statistics reported on the 10 most dangerous jobs in the United States; it was interesting to note that the fishing industry is the most dangerous, due to malfunctioning gear, inclement weather, and transportation incidents. Its fatality rate is 116 per 100,000 workers, with 29 total.

Next are the logging workers, with risk factors tied to heavy machinery, bad weather, and high altitudes. More than half of the incidents are the result of being struck by an object. Their fatality rate is 91.9 per 100,000 workers, with 59 total.

Aircraft pilots and flight engineers' fatality rate is 70.6 per 100,000 workers, with 78 total, due to transportation accidents, including crashes. Farmers and ranchers working long hours and with heavy machinery and equipment have a fatality rate of 41.4 per 100,000 workers, with 300 total. Next are mining, roofers, refuse and recyclable material collectors, truck drivers, stuntmen, and police and sheriff patrol officers.

Removing hazards is one way of improving worker protection; however in many cases it is more practical to control or manage the risks that the hazards pose. The risk is the probability or possible severity that could cause harm. The company is responsible for recognizing the hazards and risks, continually improving its occupational health and safety performance, and complying with applicable legal requirements.

Globalization (increase in competition and economic pressure), as well as the rapid development of information and communications technology (ICT), the Internet, and the shift of manufacturing to service industries, has had a huge impact on work and consequently occupational health and safety, tied to psychosocial hazards. Also restructuring and downsizing have caused increased work and tighter deadlines, adding to worker stress and fatigue. Companies have compensated by having temporary employment contracts or outsourcing to manage demands for work.

The workforce will consist of younger individuals, as many of the baby boomers will be retiring, and the make-up of the labor force will change to young immigrants, who will require additional support to integrate into the workplace. The migrant worker may have barriers to communication and training in occupational health and safety and have different cultural perceptions and attitudes concerning work and occupational risks.

In many countries, companies will try to retain the older workers to assist in mentoring the new workers, which will contribute to their economic success. Senior management needs to assess where their labor force will come from, the changes it will bring to their health and safety programs, and how they will integrate new workers in the workplace.

Not only has there been significant development in logistics and transportation—the movement of employees from one country to another—but also new technologies that have brought about changes in work practices and processes, which have generated new hazards and risks.

There has also been an increase in automation and use of powered equipment, which has reduced the need for heavy physical work, which has been replaced by other risks tied to ergonomics and exposure to electromagnetic radiation. As these changes impact businesses, changes will be needed in workplace health and safety management systems.

There are high costs associated with occupational disease, not only impoverishing workers and families but also reducing productivity and work capacity and increasing health care expenditures for countries or individuals.

According to the International Labour Organization (ILO) (April 28, 2013), in their report "The Prevention of Occupational Diseases – World Day for safety and health at work 28 April 2013," the following was outlined.

> Work-related accidents and diseases result in an annual 4% loss in global gross domestic product (GDP), or about US$2.8 trillion, in direct and indirect costs of injuries and diseases.
>
> The cost of work-related diseases in the EU has been estimated to be at least €145 billion per year. The French government estimates that compensation for ARD for the period 2001–20 will be between €27 and 37 billion, which is equivalent to €1.3 and €1.9 billion per year.
>
> In the United States, insurance companies reportedly paid $21.6 billion for asbestos-exposure cases for the period 1990–2000, in addition to the $32 billion paid out by prosecuted enterprises.
>
> In the Republic of Korea, the total economic cost of MSDs was $6.89 billion, representing 0.7% of the country's GDP in 2011.18 MSDs are estimated to cost New Zealand's health-care system over $4.71 billion per year and constitute about a quarter of the total annual health-care costs.[4]

The ILO also reported that 2.34 million workers die each year from work-related accidents and diseases. Types of diseases vary, from workplace dusts in China to musculoskeletal disorders (MSDs) and respiratory diseases in Argentina, and low-back disorders, pneumoconiosis, and mental disorders in Japan. "The US Bureau of Labor statistics reported in 2011 skin diseases, hearing loss and respiratory conditions were the three most prevalent health impairments."

Good data is limited; more than half of all countries still do not collect adequate statistics because workers in small and medium-sized enterprises, rural areas, and the informal economy represent the majority of the workforce and are outside of the systems that document, report, and compensate occupational diseases.

As stated previously, the aging population and the increasing number of temporary, casual, or part-time workers increase people's willingness to accept unsafe working conditions and impede adequate health surveillance as workers go from one job to another with various levels of exposure, making monitoring of the work environment difficult.

There is a need for a mechanism to collect proper data and to ensure management and control of hazards and risks are in place. I propose for all businesses the international standard for occupational health and safety: OHSAS 18001.

Many organizations have implemented OHSAS 18001 and have either gone for registration or self-declared their management system. It assures customers and stakeholders—government, shareholders, employees, contractors, and the community at large—that the company has an internationally recognized management system in place. I have worked with numerous organizations, establishing policies and programs that provide specific direction and delegate authority to those responsible for providing a safe and healthy workplace. An established framework that can manage and control ongoing risks and changes to processes also limits financial losses resulting from injuries.

Keeping in compliance with applicable health and safety legislation is key; having OHSAS 18001 in place ensures that you have the systems to identify legal requirements and their applicable tasks and will manage important documents and data.

Training is another key area outlined in the standard. It is important to cross-train your people, so that you have a backup plan in place if someone becomes injured and is unable to work. Monitor training and complete inspections on time and ensure that corrective actions are dealt with effectively.

The standard requires that you have audits in place to verify your management system's effectiveness and efficiencies and that any nonconformances are managed with root-cause analysis and corrective action.

The inspection programs track that you provide and maintain protective equipment, devices, and clothing, and that they are used according to standing operating procedures. Inspections also assist to ensure the safety in operating machinery and workplace operations. New technology has come into the workplace for checklist inspections to be completed on hand-held devices which store information into systems for immediate action and future tracking.

Many laws today give employees three basic rights: the right to know about hazards, the right to participate in health and safety initiatives, and the right to refuse unsafe work. There are many penalties tied to noncompliance with these legislative standards, and in some areas health and safety officers have the power to inspect workplaces, investigate workplace complaints and accidents, and issue orders for noncompliance, which can be very costly for an organization.

Having open communication is important, whether you are required by law to have a health and safety committee or you have a smaller company and conduct regular meetings with your people. Inform them of hazards within their areas. Encourage them to suggest improvements for the workplace either through their supervisors or directly to management, as they understand their work area the best and can recognize areas of concern and how they can be changed. Investigate these opportunities and any reported unsafe conditions. These are usually outlined in minutes; however, it is better for tracking if these are documented in your corrective action system, ensuring that action is taken without delay.

OHSAS 18001 is not an ISO standard, but a specification developed by the British Standards Institute (BSI) to guide organizations in managing effective occupational health and safety (OH&S).

OCCUPATIONAL HEALTH AND SAFETY MANAGEMENT SYSTEM PRINCIPLES*

- Leadership
- Continual improvement
- System approach to management
- Compliance with legal and other requirements
- Performance evaluation
- Management of resources
- Operational control
- Emergency preparedness and response

---

* Neither British Standards Institute nor ISO has outlined principles for occupational health and safety.

Leadership

Focus: Health and Safety—Prevention of Injury and Ill Health*

Top management recognizes the priority of occupational health and safety management as an integral part of its business success. It leads by establishing vision, policy, objectives, programs, and practices to ensure its commitment to prevention of injury and ill health by controlling its risks and improving its OH&S performance.

Senior management and the board set the leadership for a safe and healthy workplace within the organization by making a commitment

---

* The following quotes on principles are from Pilot Performance Resources Management Inc.'s speaking series on "Driving Business Sustainability," helping companies maintain and succeed in their business in all markets through all circumstances.

to prevention of injury and ill health in its policies, ensuring the identification of risks of its processes, materials, equipment, and activities and putting in place objectives contributing to the safety and health.

Management has a responsibility to eliminate or minimize risks to personnel and other interested parties who could be exposed to hazards associated with its activities. Management can lead by sharing its vision and commitment to building an incident and injury-free work environment and integrating health and safety with other roles and responsibilities. By communicating continuously the established limits it puts on risk taking and the value of safety during meetings and training, and in posters, and involving employees during design, implementation, and corrective actions, the organization will make health and safety performance transparent throughout the organization for all key stakeholders.

To reinforce a strong health and safety culture within the organization, employee involvement is crucial. Employees are empowered to challenge unsafe acts and continually work to improve occupational health and safety programs and performance. Workers have the right to work in a safe and healthy working environment and have the right to refuse work if it is unsafe.

Workers give input to operational controls they are working in. Top management sets its policy statement by considering the following:

1. Who is the health and safety management system directed toward?
   a. An organization needs to take into consideration present employees, new and young workers, temporary workers, contractors, people with disabilities, visitors, maintenance workers, the public, etc.
2. What risks does the health and safety management work toward?
   a. Identify your significant occupational health and safety (OH&S) hazards by doing a risk assessment, commit to prevention of injury and ill health, and continually improve OH&S management system and performance. The use of competent expert advice may be required for risk assessment.

    b. The legal emphasis has been on worker's right to:

        i. Know hazards and risks

        ii. Participate in health and safety activities and worker-management committees

        iii. Refuse hazardous work

3. What controls are in place for operations?

    a. Determine controls or changes to existing controls. Review design of work areas, processes, installations, and procedures.

    b. The following hierarchy is outlined by OHSAS 18001:

        i. elimination

        ii. substitution

        iii. engineering controls

        iv. signs/warnings and/or administrative controls

        v. personal protective equipment

    c. Innovation: Workers are encouraged to be creative in coming up with solutions to health and safety.

The board of directors, as mentioned earlier, should be aware of the risks tied to the operational controls of business operations. This would include acceptable risks tied to its legal obligations and its own OH&S policy.

The company's occupational health and safety policy sets out the company's commitment to prevention of injury and ill health and continual improvement in its management and performance. The policy needs to be communicated to persons working under the control of the organization with the intent that they are made aware of the health and safety commitments by all.

The policy statement needs to be reviewed periodically (usually yearly) to ensure that it remains relevant to the organization.

Objectives and programs need to be tied to the identified hazards and risks at the organization, prioritizing and controlling them through operational controls.

Actions must be taken within the organization to minimize consequences of occupational hazards, and information is vital for dissemination of information on effective programs and policies related to identified hazards. Surveillance of the workplace and identification of hazards through a risk assessment are the first step, and then internal controls help the organization make informed decisions about the level of risk that it wants to take. Monitoring procedures and compliance requirements through inspections and audits assists the organization in managing effectively and efficiently.

Training is key for top management to provide, as workers need to know not only about their work responsibilities but also about the hazards and how to protect themselves and their coworkers.

GKN

GKN is an engineering global group and has registered to ISO 14001 and OHSAS 18001. This company has 48,000 people worldwide, with 250 years of heritage in 32 countries. It has four divisions: Automotive (driveline-systems and solutions), Powder Metallurgy (world's largest manufacturer of sintered components), Aerospace (first-tier supplier to the global aviation industry), and Land Systems (leading supplier of power management solutions and services).

Its commitment in health and safety and environment starts with its values and the GKN Code: "We will provide employees with a healthy and safe working environment. We will play our part in the protection of the environment in both the operation of our facilities and the design of our products." Its OH&S policy statement outlines its commitment to legislation in each jurisdiction it is in and its pursuit of "zero accidents."

One of its key principles is that health and safety considerations are intrinsic to the adoption and introduction of any new technique or process. Another is that new hires receive training and appropriate refresher training; that commitment to ongoing training ensures that workers are able to undertake the work safely from the outset and throughout their GKN career.

Its policy statement outlines its principles, practice, measures, and metrics and includes a statement on assurance, which is to have regular reviews of health and safety arrangements and performance and external audit of its procedures to ensure compliance with policy and relevant legislation.[5]

Companies can try many innovative ways to lead, by having each board director become a champion or mentor in one aspect related to occupational health and safety, or having senior management do safety tours and interact with workers, or rebranding their corporate image to include occupational health and safety. Companies can work together with their industry associations and insurance companies to implement programs to improve health and safety and reduce claims.

An important function of leadership is to ensure that the values of the organization relating to policy, risk management, and internal control are communicated from the top. A code of conduct can support the types of behaviors the organization wants and outline the consequences of not following it. Management then needs to follow up with applicable actions regarding the violations.

Awards and recognition of positive performance also helps improve morale. Has any company offered an award for "bad practice"? That might be a new spin on presenting awards. Individual personal performance reviews tied to key objectives and targets and maintaining operational controls would assist in business success by making individuals accountable.

Assess & Reflect #24

LEADERSHIP

Focus: Health and Safety—Prevention of Injury and Ill Health

❶ As a leader, what questions do you ask your people in order to look at new opportunities, new solutions, and profitability/performance/productivity?

❷ As a leader, do you ask "what is missing" from your occupational health and safety management system in order to improve it? Do you humbly ask your management team for input to your biggest challenges? Do you stand up for what is best for your employees? Are you unafraid to put your job on the line when the board of directors is of the opposite mindset?

❸ What is your reputation for leading your organization? Are you a good champion or leader? Why do you think you are?

❹ What did the results of your organization's baseline risk assessment show about your organization?

❺ Have you changed any processes and programs or do you have any new projects going on within your organization? Did you review the risks tied to these areas? Have they been added to your baseline risk assessment?

❻ Do investors trust your reporting? Do you have transparency in your reporting?

❼ To be a great leader you need to remain competitive. How do you do this within your industry?

❽ What innovations have you put in place to lead your organization in occupational health and safety? What are your priorities?

❾ What objectives and targets do you presently have in place to improve occupational health and safety? What is your focus for this area? What are your possibilities?

❿ As a leader, have you set out for the organization what is essential versus what is important at the time?

⓫ Is transparency part of your leadership principles? How do you share what your organization knows publicly? Do you encourage and reward sharing by managers, employees, and customers? Do you treat managers and workers with respect?

Act

LEADERSHIP

Focus: Health and Safety—Prevention of Injury and Ill Health

_____
_____
_____
_____
_____
_____
_____
_____
_____
_____
_____
_____
_____
_____
_____
_____
_____
_____
_____
_____
_____
_____
_____
_____
_____
_____
_____

Continual Improvement

Focus: Health and Safety—Prevention of Injury and Ill Health

Forecast and assess challenges and opportunities for ongoing continual improvement in prevention of injury and ill health, achieving ongoing improvement in occupational health and safety practices and performance.

Occupational health and safety needs the total commitment of an organization's board and high-level management—senior management—not just line management and employees in directly being involved in its continual improvement.

Senior management's main tasks in leadership are to forecast and assess challenges and opportunities for ongoing continual improvement in prevention of injury and ill health, developing its vision, strategy, policies, and contingency plans and at the same time focusing on long-term profitability.

As outlined in the environmental section, continual improvement is a journey and an ongoing commitment by top management, requiring employee engagement and stakeholder support, and it needs to be applied wherever the company is conducting business.

Rana Plaza–Bangladesh

In July 2013, the *Guardian* did a story on the Rana Plaza building in Bangladesh that collapsed, putting factory working conditions under the global eye. IndustriALL, an international union group, is working to tackle fire safety and building security in Bangladesh and developing a similar agreement in Pakistan and China, which face greater workplace risks. More than half of the clothing factories inspected in Bangladesh and Pakistan fail to meet fire standards, according to Sedex, a nonprofit group. In both countries safety issues include lack of alarms, blocked fire exits, long working hours, low wages, and child labor.

Wal-Mart

Wal-Mart, which ranks at the top of the Fortune 500 companies, has more than 10,500 stores in 27 countries and employs more than 2.2 million associates worldwide. It has truly been a leader in sustainability, corporate philanthropy, and employment opportunities. In April 2013 Wal-Mart committed $1.6 million to the Institute of Sustainable Communities (ISC), a U.S.-based NGO, to establish an Environment, Health and Safety Academy in Bangladesh. The Swedish International Development Agency (SIDA) is also a partner in providing support for the new academy. The focus of the academy will be on fire safety, water management, and enhancing gender equity in the workplace and creating professional opportunities for Bangladeshi women.

With this initiative, Wal-Mart is taking a stand to raise standards and improve fire safety within its supply chain. In January 2013, Wal-Mart instituted a zero-tolerance policy for unauthorized subcontracting and strengthened fire safety standards in Bangladesh, where it is conducting electrical, building, and fire safety assessments. Prior to Bangladesh, Wal-Mart supported a similar academy in China, providing financial resources, technical expertise, and advice.

Jay Jorgensen, SVP and global chief compliance officer of Wal-Mart, said, "Transparency is key to the success of this effort."[6] He said that it is crucial to work together—industry, government, workers, and NGOs—to make changes and increase and improve the quality of life of the women and men in the company's supply chain.

The principle of continual improvement is crucial to the ability of the business to sustain its operations. Companies depend on people in Bangladesh to make their products.

It is interesting that Wal-Mart works at continual improvement in Bangladesh, but in August of 2013, OHS Online reported that "OSHA announced a corporate-wide settlement to improve safety and health conditions in 2,857 Wal-Mart and Sam's Club stores in the United States. The settlement specifies trash compactors must remain locked while not in use and may not be operated except while under the supervision of a trained manager or another trained, designated monitor. Wal-Mart will strengthen its procedures to ensure employees do not handle undiluted cleaning chemicals and ensure protective protocol is in place."[7]

A Journey

As I said earlier, continual improvement in health and safety is a journey. Hopefully companies will learn and improve as they go and there will not be fatalities in the process.

By improving design and work practices and systems, you can improve in these two areas:

1. **Health hazards:** Chemical (toxic, carcinogenic, flammable); biological (bacteria, viruses, blood, and mold); physical (noise, temperature, vibration, radiation, lifting); ergonomic (repetitive motion injury); psychosocial (violence in the workplace); psychological (working conditions, fatigue, stress)

2. **Safety hazards:** Mechanical (machine part guarding, moving parts, ladders, lock-out); other (handling of tools, equipment, working at heights, confined space, falls); special (weather, earthquakes, tornado); fire and explosion (fuel sources)

Measurable objectives, data, and reporting (such as dashboards) provide valuable timely information so decision makers can analyze and improve OH&S performance. When establishing and reviewing the OH&S objectives, take into account the legal and other requirements of the countries in which you operate.

As indicated earlier, some countries do not have standards in place, and no matter where you live, everyone has the right to a safe environment. The organization needs to do a proper risk assessment of the areas in which it is operating, ensuring a high standard of health and safety for all.

A proper management system structure in these countries would ensure that the framework for assessing risks is in place, as well as setting in place controls for these risks. A corrective action process is required to manage nonconformances and is ideal for continual improvement, as it assesses root causes and requires plans of action, which are then verified for completion.

CONTINUAL IMPROVEMENT

FOCUS: HEALTH AND SAFETY—PREVENTION OF INJURY AND ILL HEALTH

1. In what areas has your company improved in occupational health and safety?
   a. Design
   b. Process
   c. Work practices
   d. Other
2. What processes do you have in place to manage continual improvement?
3. How often does your board of directors meet to review continual improvement in your organization? How often does senior management meet to review continual improvement?
4. What inputs does top management review for continual improvement?
   a. Results of internal audits, compliance audits, third-party registration audits, supplier audits
   b. Communication from external interested parties (government, complaints)
   c. Review of status of objectives and targets
   d. Changing circumstances and laws
   e. Recommendations for improvement
   f. Status of incident investigations and corrective and preventive actions
5. How has your organization contributed to outside improvement of occupational health and safety?
6. Is your leadership style such that your organization is flexible and has the ability to manage change? Do you have a change-management procedure in place?
7. Do your workers participate in identifying opportunitites for continual improvement to prevent injury and ill health? What innovative ideas did they come up with in the last year?
8. What improvements have you made in health and safety in emerging countries?

Act

CONTINUAL IMPROVEMENT

FOCUS: HEALTH AND SAFETY—PREVENTION OF INJURY AND ILL HEALTH

System Approach to Management

Focus: Health and Safety—Prevention of Injury and Ill Health

A system approach is identifying, understanding, and managing integrated and interdependent processes and their risks that contribute to the organization's occupational health and safety management system's effectiveness and performance.

The international standard for occupational health and safety management system is OHSAS 18001 (see Figure 8.1). Organizations can choose to have their company registered to this standard through a certification process by independent accredited bodies (registrars) or

FIGURE 8.1

Occupational Health and Safety Management System Model

Source: Pilot Performance Resources Management Inc.

Note: OHSAS 18001:2007 will be replaced by ISO 45001:2016 (refer to Part 3 Annex SL).

self-declare their management system to the standard, having a third party audit the system. This ensures verification of the management system through the third party's audit. Before a management system goes for registration the organization needs to conduct an internal audit and management review. The internal audit can be done by your own trained employees or a third-party, contracted internal auditor.

An organization can utilize Pilot's Three-Step Process—"Identify, Insure and Improve"™—for implementing its occupational health and safety management system to the standard (the three steps apply to any management system implementation process, e.g., ISO 14001, ISO 9001) and then review it through the internal audit for each process area.

Assess & Reflect #26

SYSTEM APPROACH TO MANAGEMENT

Focus: Health and Safety—Prevention of Injury and Ill Health

1. What criteria do you manage your occupational health and safety to?
2. Have you implemented your management system to OHSAS 18001? What version (year)?
3. What other management systems do you have in place?
   a. Quality management system—ISO 9001   Yes   No
   b. Environmental management system—
      ISO 14001   Yes   No
   c. Process or job control management system   Yes   No
   d. Inventory system   Yes   No
   e. Accounting system: _____   Yes   No
   f. Other: _____
4. To what extent have you integrated your occupational health and safety activities with the following: Partially, fully, not at all
   a. Environmental management
   b. Quality management
   c. Integrated management system with quality, environment, health and safety
   d. Other: _____

SYSTEM APPROACH TO MANAGEMENT

FOCUS: HEALTH AND SAFETY—PREVENTION OF INJURY AND ILL HEALTH

_____

_____

_____

_____

_____

_____

_____

_____

_____

_____

_____

_____

_____

_____

_____

_____

_____

_____

_____

_____

_____

_____

_____

_____

_____

Compliance with Legal and Other Requirements

Focus: Health and Safety—Prevention of Injury and Ill Health

Compliance with applicable occupational health and safety legislation, regulations, guidelines, and policies is a permanent objective of the organization to ensure that adequate systems, practices, and controls are in place.

Countries vary in their approaches to occupational health and safety legislation and regulations, along with their enforcement and incentives to be in compliance.

In the European Union, some countries promote occupational health and safety by providing public monies as subsides, grants, or financing and have created tax system incentives.

In the United States, since the 1970s, OSHA, in the U.S. Department of Labor, is responsible for developing and enforcing workplace health and safety regulations, whereas the National Institute for Occupational Safety and Health (NIOSH) focuses on research, information, education, and training.

In Canada, since 1996 workers have been covered by federal and provincial codes, depending on the sectors they work in. The Canadian Centre for Occupational Health and Safety (CCOHS) is an agency of the Canadian government that focuses on promoting safe and healthy workplaces to help prevent work-related injuries and illnesses.

It has only been since 2002 that regulations were put in place in the People's Republic of China, under the Ministry of Health and the State Administration of Work Safety. India also is a country where huge opportunities to utilize the economical workforce for manufacturing are available for companies.

Argentina, China, Finland, Malaysia, Portugal, Thailand, the United Kingdom, and Vietnam have established national OSH programs, with prevention of occupational diseases as a priority, and Lao PDR, Papua New Guinea, and South Africa have taken further steps by including prevention of occupational diseases in their national OSH policies and programs, as reported by the ILO.

The ILO has provided assistance in shaping and updating national lists of occupational diseases to governments, employers, and worker's organizations through advisory and consultation services. It sees the road ahead with a focus on prevention and treatment of occupational diseases, as well as the improvement of recording.

In addition to existing hazards, new hazards are emerging, driven by both technological and social changes and by the global economic crisis. Millions of workers are exposed to hazardous working conditions without recourse to any system of protection, and therefore prevention is key and more effective than treatment and rehabilitation. The future may bring the integration of prevention of occupational diseases into labor inspection programs for mining, construction, and agriculture.

In emerging countries growth rates are high and populations are dense, and therefore low-cost, low-knowledge workers are available. These countries bear a large percentage of the burden of occupational disease and injury. There is no single authority or mechanism in place for ensuring reporting of spills and accidents and no penalty for non-compliance. Their regulations in many industries are not evolved or de-tailed and do not require inspections or monitoring systems.

It is the CEOs, presidents, and leaders of global organizations who need to recognize OHS as a strategic enabler of sustained economic growth in these countries, given that legal requirements are not in place. What does the company value? Business performance is not measured with respect to health and safety; however, a safe work environment may go a long way to increase the productivity of employees in these countries.

If health and safety is a core value of a company, then it should con-tribute to the functioning of the entire organization and not be changed or compromised when working in emerging countries. All workers within the organization need to work in a safe environment.

Some of the laws we take for granted are not required in other countries, such as wearing safety hats and seat belts and using personal protective wear when handling chemicals and hazardous materials.

A management system adhering to OHSAS 18001 requires companies not only to identify their legal and other requirements but also to define the applicable tasks tied to the requirements. To verify that a company is following its legal requirements, it must perform a compliance audit. In some companies compliance internal audits are conducted by the head office; in other companies this activity is contracted out to third-party auditors.

In North America, health and safety is supported by inspections and fines that could put smaller companies out of business, ranging from thousands to hundreds of thousands of dollars.

With the Internet, Facebook, YouTube, and the ease of taking videos with phones, evidence related to accidents and incidents is easily documented and displayed immediately, and companies need preventative measures in place to ensure legal requirements are followed.

Assess & Reflect #27

COMPLIANCE WITH LEGAL

FOCUS: HEALTH AND SAFETY—PREVENTION OF INJURY AND ILL HEALTH

1. Has the organization identified its legal and other occupational health and safety obligations and associated tasks?

2. What "other" requirements does the organization need to be in compliance with besides the regulatory requirements (industry codes of practice, union agreements, temporary work agreements, etc.)? Has your organization outlined the tasks tied to these requirements? Are the requirements included in the compliance review or audit?

3. Has your organization outlined allocation of responsibilities for senior managers, managers, supervisors, employees, contractors, visitors, and occupational health and safety committees?

4. Do you have designated individual(s) to handle legal requirements in your organization? How often do they report to top management?

5. What education/promotion/awareness is provided for managers, supervisors, employees, and others about the importance of compliance with specific legislation and legal requirements and the risks of noncompliance?

6. What were the results of your last occupational health and safety compliance review or audit? Was it done by outside resources?

7. Do you have a monitoring and reporting mechanism to provide information to appropriate managers regarding noncompliance and corrective action? Do you have a separate system for reporting compliance issues or do you manage all your nonconformances within one process area with categories for nonconformances?

8. Have government officials visited your facility? When? What were the results of this visit? Was it documented?

9. Does your organization perform business in countries where there are no regulations for occupational health and safety? What is your policy regarding those countries?

10. How has your organization contributed in emerging countries to improving occupational health and safety for workers?

11. What hazardous conditions exist in countries presently where you are carrying on business? How is this documented and controlled for the workers who report to your organization?

Act

COMPLIANCE WITH LEGAL AND OTHER

FOCUS: HEALTH AND SAFETY—PREVENTION OF INJURY AND ILL HEALTH

_____

_____

_____

_____

_____

_____

_____

_____

_____

_____

_____

_____

_____

_____

_____

_____

_____

_____

_____

_____

_____

_____

_____

_____

_____

_____

_____

Performance Evaluation

Monitoring and measurement of occupational health and safety hazards, risks, and performance indicators form the basis of continual improvement. External unattached assessment, as well as internal, will identify business improvement opportunities and shortcomings and provide unbiased intelligence. Effective decisions are based on the analysis of data and information.

Top management is responsible for performance monitoring, from monitoring the extent to which the organization's occupational health and safety plans and objectives are being met, to monitoring the effectiveness of controls. Then there is the monitoring of conformance and compliance with the organization's management system programs and operational criteria.

Reactive measures are also monitored regarding ill health, incidents (accidents, near-misses), and other historical evidence of deficient performance. A low accident rate does not necessary mean that risks are being effectively controlled.

Effective monitoring of the organization's hazards and its control of risks needs to be planned and implemented. Line management is responsible for monitoring these two areas, active and reactive systems.

Active systems are the design, development, production, and operation of management arrangements, which are tied to documented procedures and objectives (projects) and can be verified through review of risk assessments (functioning as intended or updated), inspections of processes and equipment, sampling (noise, air, dust), maintenance, calibration, audits (compliance/conformance), and management reviews.

Having performance criteria in place is important, as what gets measured gets done. The monitoring needs to be proportional to the hazard profile for the organization.

Reactive systems include the monitoring of incidents/accidents and ill health. This requires an open approach to reporting from workers and a documented procedure for handling nonconformance or noncompliance (legal), investigating the area for corrective action, preventing recurrence, and, if required, restoring compliance as soon as possible.

This may be controlled through an accident/incident investigation process or the company's nonconformance/corrective action process system, which is tied to its management system identifying the category as an accident/incident. This would put all nonconformances, including those for noncompliance, in one reporting system that can be sorted by categories or areas.

It is important to review not only who was involved or injured and what and where it occurred but also the root cause of the incident/ accident and how a similar incident can be prevented, as well as the continual improvement of the situation.

As part of the process, look at where this information is kept and review the risk assessment log, where the list of all company's hazards have been identified, to ensure that it has been updated, as well as the documents and training applicable to the incident/accident. Ensure that the results of the investigations have been communicated in a timely manner.

Inspections are an ongoing task, both scheduled and unscheduled, ensuring the identification of hazards; after inspections the hazards should be eliminated or controlled. As mentioned earlier, the use of hand-held devices for inspections assists greatly in data management and communicating results immediately to all persons for actions or review.

If equipment is required to monitor and measure performance, then calibration and maintenance procedures need to be in place and records kept of activities.

Top management can improve the organization's overall approach to health and safety by combining the monitoring of performance with audit reports. An organization can do its own compliance audit or review or contract with an outside consulting company to ensure that it is meeting applicable legal requirements.

The internal and third-party audit process (auditors independent from the audited activity) assists the organization in reviewing and verifying the effectiveness and efficiency of its processes, "closing the loop" to reduce risks and continually improve the organization's management system.

It is through the review of monitoring and measurement that continual improvement can take place in redesign, amendment, or changes to the company's objectives, processes, or procedures. It is crucial through the change management process to share results with workers to engage them in the successes and failures of the system. The company can improve performance by emphasizing positive reinforcement and engagement.

A positive health and safety culture can be achieved by benchmarking with other similar organizations rather than measuring failure against accident data.

Reviews are a continuous process undertaken at different levels in the organization during routine activities, inspections, assessment of new projects/plans, audit results, etc. The action items need to have defined responsibilities, tasks, and deadlines for completion, which are then monitored. Companies continue to have many projects in place, and priorities to be assessed according to the degree of risks involved, legal compliance requirements, and the availability of resources.

Boards of directors or senior management need to be kept informed and, if required, alerted to relevant health and safety risk management objectives and any issues, ensuring that the management systems are in place and remain effective. One of the board members could be selected as the health and safety champion.

It is important to ensure that health and safety performance is reviewed at least annually by the board and that the policy statement reflects the board's current priorities. When significant health and safety failures happen within the organization the board should be kept informed and review the outcome of the investigations into their causes.

Boards can be kept more actively involved by providing positive feedback, demonstrating gratitude when improvement is identified and implemented, and participating as a stakeholder in the recognition activities for workers at lunches and awards ceremonies.

A demonstration of a corporation's commitment to health and safety and its performance monitoring can be published in annual reports.

Assess & Reflect #28

PERFORMANCE EVALUATION

Focus: Health and Safety—Prevention of Injury and Ill Health

1. Do you know how well your company is performing in health and safety? How is the performance measured?
2. Do you keep your board directors and senior management informed about your performance? How?
3. Is the board active in reviewing your occupational health and safety performance? Do they ensure that you have a management system in place and it is effective, and that risk assessment is part of evaluating your performance? Do you report to the board about health and safety?
4. Has your board or senior management appointed someone at the director level to ensure safety and health risk management issues are properly addressed? Is the person competent to do so? If not, what support is given to the individual?
5. Are your measurements for performance good enough? Are your controls for risks good enough? What data supports this?
6. Do you know if your company complies with applicable legal regulations/laws? If you don't meet the requirements, what can be done or what is being done for due diligence?
7. Does your organization carry out internal audits related to occupational health and safety? How often? Is the time frame tied to your organization's occupational health and safety risks adequate?
8. When did you last review and revise your occupational health and safety policy statement?
9. Do you set high expectations and performance standards for your management team?

Act

PERFORMANCE EVALUATION

Focus: Monitoring and Measurement of Prevention of Injury and Ill Health

_____

_____

_____

_____

_____

_____

_____

_____

_____

_____

_____

_____

_____

_____

_____

_____

_____

_____

_____

_____

_____

_____

_____

_____

Management of Resources

Focus: Health and Safety—Prevention of Injury and Ill Health

Top management ensures adequate and effective management of our resources: human resources (labor, training, competence, communication/ participation/consultation), specialized skills, organizational infrastructure, technology, documentation, and financial resources.

Responsibility for health and safety risks ultimately rests with top management; regardless of whether you are a big or small company, you are legally required to ensure your workplace is a safe and healthy place to work.

Senior management ensures not only the design and implementation of its policies and risk strategies but also the internal controls tied to the risks and the assignment of resources to establish, implement, maintain, and improve its OH&S management system.

Resources include human resources, specialized skills, organizational infrastructure, technology, and financial resources. All those with management responsibility shall demonstrate their commitment to the continual improvement of OHS&S performance, as well as workers; however, senior management is responsible for the risk controls, not line management. The people responsible for controls also need to be defined.

The implementation and continual improvement of the system are supported through communication, participation, and consultation through team meetings with employees, contractors, and stakeholders.

The company provides education and training and equips employees with proper equipment to avoid unsafe situations and the ability to respond to emergencies and incidents.

When work is to be done that could endanger a worker, the employer ensures that the worker is competent or is working under the supervision of someone who is competent. So what is competent? Competency as described by OHSAS 18001 includes appropriate education, training, or experience to perform the work.

Managers need to be competent to understand how changes in the organization's processes, systems, activities, or objectives can impact its risks so that appropriate controls can be put in place and monitored for their effectiveness.

Many organizations have health and safety committees composed of management and workers who act as an advisory body and who are mutually committed to improving health and safety conditions in the workplace. They identify workplace risks and develop recommendations for the employer to address. Regular meetings and inspections take place and written recommendations are given to the employer.

Individual responsibilities include the responsibility of health and safety activities under their control. Participation by employees supports the commitment and control of risks. Therefore health and safety becomes everyone's business, from risk identification to partnering for prevention through the company's processes and procedures to management of nonconforming activities, accident/incident investigation, and reassessments. Involvement of people from all levels is essential and the need to be innovative in health and safety matters.

Documentation of the company's policies, objectives, and management system is outlined and controlled in a manual. The manual includes: the scope of the management system, an outline of the interaction of its processes, and references to applicable procedures, work instructions, data-bases where information can be located. The control of documents and records provides support and due diligence for the organization on its occupational health and safety.

Training is provided to new workers, transferred workers, existing workers, and contractors to ensure they have an understanding of the company's policies, its processes, hazards, and applicable operating procedures and that they are properly equipped to perform services at the company. Training or communication is provided to all, including visitors, concerning emergency preparedness plans.

Success in improving occupational health and safety is widely attributed to communication with all stakeholders, as well as knowledge sharing, feedback, and accurate reporting.

Assess & Reflect #29

RESOURCES

Focus: Health & Safety—Prevention of Injury and Ill Health

❶ What are your important resources within your organization? Are they adequate? What percentage of your employees will be retiring in next three to five years? What plans do you have in place for their replacement? What plans do you have in place to capture the knowledge of supervisors/managers who are leaving?

❷ Is there worker involvement in the development and review of OH&S policies, practices, and objectives?

❸ Were workers involved in the hazard identification and risk assessments, as well as the determination of controls? Are workers involved in incident investigation?

❹ Are board members and top management generally aware of the authority and responsibility of the board? Are the board's decisions implemented satisfactorily and communicated throughout the organization?

❺ How do you or other managers in your organization communicate your core values or guiding principles?

❻ What type of communication is done with contractors and visitors about:
   a. Hazards within the organization
   b. Rules tied to environment, health, and safety
   c. Emergency preparedness

❼ Are you asking your management team to do important tasks that they are not capable of doing correctly? Do you need to invest in training?

❽ How do you demonstrate that your workers are competent to do their jobs? What records are kept to verify this?

❾ Are role descriptions and authorities clear and known in the organization? Are changes to personnel kept up in documentation?

❿ Is there clear and effective communication with management and workers and in general do stakeholders know what is going on?

⓫ Does training take into account risk, responsibility, ability, language skills, and literacy?

Act

RESOURCES

FOCUS: PREVENTION OF INJURY AND ILL HEALTH

_____

_____

_____

_____

_____

_____

_____

_____

_____

_____

_____

_____

_____

_____

_____

_____

_____

_____

_____

_____

_____

_____

_____

_____

Operational Control

Focus: Health and Safety—Prevention of Injury and Ill Health

Establish, implement, monitor, measure, and maintain with change management control of functions, activities, and processes associated with hazards to manage occupational health and safety risks.

Emphasis on financial reporting alone distracts top management from ensuring that operational controls are in place and functioning. Many business failures have identified insufficient controlled risks at the operational level that have caused problems before the financials were even prepared.

Top management leads by creating and promoting a safe workplace, by ensuring that process activities that were identified to have hazards and risks or health and safety legal requirements have clear roles and responsibilities tied to operations, as that enables a business to function effectively and efficiently in its activities, products, and services.

Internal operational controls support the organization's objectives in managing its occupational health and safety risks, while complying with regulations and organizational policies.

Operational controls may be in the form of operating procedures, change management, controls related to purchased goods, equipment, and services, controls tied to contractors and other visitors, preventative maintenance, etc., which contribute to the prevention of pollution.

All employees can take a leadership role in health and safety. As well, there needs to be adequate field supervision to provide prompt feedback to employee concerns.

The organization ensures that the hazards not only within the organization but also outside the workplace that are capable of adversely affecting the health and safety of persons under the control of the organization within the workplace are considered not only when establishing and implementing its occupational health and safety management system but also when it is maintained. An organization needs to look at its design and development of new projects and facilities, its ongoing operations, and maintenance and change management activities.

Controls are put in place for prevention of injury and illness through operational controls. When determining controls, OHSAS 18001 outlines the following hierarchy: elimination, substitution, engineering controls, signage/warnings and/or administrative controls, and personal protective equipment.

Inspections aid in critical examination of the workplace by identifying and recording hazards for corrective action. Your joint occupational health and safety workplace committee can help plan, conduct, report, and monitor your inspections.

You may also include environment as part of your health and safety when doing inspections. When doing inspections it is helpful to view them by the process areas, by utilizing plant floor plans and drawings and understanding the main risks to inspect within that process area.

The use of photographs assists in reviews of hazards in operations. It is critical to have the details outlined properly in the reports, showing exact locations, situations, and characteristics. Monitoring and follow-up should be done from these inspections to ensure timely corrective actions are in place and to see if there are any trends that need to be addressed.

Your maintenance department is very aware of what operations require attention. They can provide feedback and input for equipment and process changes or requirements.

Research can be done on the types of typical hazards that apply to occupational health and safety and to your industry. Some studies indicate that the greatest injuries are sprains and strains. Your company can investigate any applicable injuries your company has had and look to areas to improve the use of alternate equipment, methods, or processes.

Assess & Reflect #30

OPERATIONAL CONTROL

Focus: Health and Safety—Prevention of Injury and Ill Health

❶ What operational controls are in place for purchased goods, equipment, and services? First, is consideration given to potential health and safety risks prior to purchasing work equipment? Do(es):
   a. Chemical purchases have material safety data sheets.
   b. New work equipment complies with the relevant legal requirements for safe design and construction.
   c. New equipment has manuals for safe installation, use, and maintenance

❷ Have you put any of the following controls in place?
   a. Replaced a substance with a less hazardous substance
   b. Used mechanical aids to reduce or eliminate manual handling
   c. Adapted work areas by adjusting height tables or chairs (ergonomics)
   d. Safeguarded machinery (switches that turn off the machine if someone tries to gain access to dangerous areas—adequately placed for use)

❸ What results related to your facility did your insurance report outline? How do they compare to the results from internal audits and inspections?

❹ What controls do you have in place for the following risks?
   a. Hazardous materials
   b. Fire
   c. Radiation
   d. Electric shock, electrical awareness, electrical control, lockout/tag out
   e. Working at heights (fall arrest, elevated power platforms)
   f. Confined space
   g. Cranes and hoists
   h. Machine guarding
   i. Psychosocial
   j. Health (noise, respiratory, dermatitis)

❺ What operational controls are in place for the following?
   a. Change management
   b. Contractors

(continued)

Assess & Reflect (continued)

    c. Visitors

    d. Preventative maintenance

6 What input has your maintenance department given for improvement in operational controls for safety?

7 What input has your quality department given for improvement for operations?

8 What input have your contractors given for improvement for operations?

9 What was the most innovative change made in production or service provision at the company in the last year for health and safety?

OPERATIONAL CONTROL

Focus: Health and Safety—Prevention of Injury and Ill Health

_____

_____

_____

_____

_____

_____

_____

_____

_____

_____

_____

_____

_____

_____

_____

_____

_____

_____

_____

_____

_____

_____

_____

Emergency Preparedness and Response

Focus: Health and Safety—Prevention of Injury and Ill Health

The organization is responsible for ensuring that it is prepared for and can respond to emergency situations and accidents and prevent or mitigate associated adverse occupational health and safety consequences.

The environmental movement and labor leaders have contributed to changes in occupational health and safety. Major tragedies in the mining industry brought about groups such as OSHA in the United States.

Not only is labor a powerful force to build products, but also it kept the wheels of war going. An expression used back in the 1930s–40s was "save a day" which meant work to save workers so that they could keep the planes flying for the "freedom" of tomorrow. Do we have the freedom if we have unsafe work?

Does your company put corporate financing ahead of safety? Has your corporate office required operating costs to be reduced by a certain percentage? Disasters don't just happen; they are a chain of critical events caused by design flaws, human error, or terrorism.

British Petroleum

The refineries owned by British Petroleum (BP) have had disasters causing loss of lives in Texas, even though there are strict guidelines in the oil industry. When this type of emergency happens, investigators are brought in to review what has happened.

Due to global terrorism, FBI agents were the first to investigate, as the oil industry would be a main target for terrorists. The U.S. Chemical Safety and Hazard Investigation Board (CSB) was then called in once terrorism was ruled out to investigate this disaster, bringing in Don Holmstrom, who is known in the media as the safety evangelist.

After lengthy investigation, reviews of photographs, videos, data from the hard drives, electronic records from the control room, and interviews with employees, it was found that the causes of this disaster were related to a number of areas:

1. **Slack operating practices.** If your company is operating more than one shift, then consideration has to be given to proper hand-over to the next shift related to operations, as well as any monitoring that has taken place and its results and the impact it will have on the next shift. Communication is essential. Many companies have work instructions in place and they are not being followed; the workers are going by common practices, and when an investigation or audit finds these occurrences, it is management's responsibility to investigate the issues at hand and manage the corrective actions.

2. **Poorly maintained equipment.** It is advisable for managers to review their work order system to review areas of concern, whether these areas are being dealt with, and why. Is the equipment part of a high-risk area? If a company is aware of new designs that would eliminate risk in its operations but they do not put them into practice, can they be held accountable? Is management by finance or by safety?

3. **Inadequate supervision.** A supervisor left a post at a critical moment and the back-up person had never handled start-up before. Are your backup people trained to take over areas if your supervisors are not available for any reason?

In this Texas oil disaster, many people were killed in a trailer that was located close to the blow-down area. When the risks tied to the location of the trailer were reviewed, the severity of the risk was tied to the length of time individuals would be in that trailer, which was close to the hazardous area. It is important to review the logic of your organization's assessment of risks.

Emergency preparedness is the act of being prepared for an unexpected disaster, to minimize injuries and property damage. Organizations are required to identify the potential for emergency situations, looking at worst-case scenarios and how they will respond to such situations.

This may be a natural disaster tied to a hurricane, tornado, earthquake, flooding, or a deadly influenza outbreak, workplace violence, chemical spill, gas leak, or transportation accident. As outlined in OHSAS 18001, the organization shall respond to actual emergency situations by preventing or mitigating adverse occupational health and safety consequences. Your emergency procedures must comply with applicable legal requirements, including fire codes and emergency response acts.

When implementing your emergency preparedness plans, know who your neighbors are. They may have more of an impact on you then you do on them. If you have railways that go past your industry, do you have contact information for reaching them in an event of an emergency?

Many organizations hire security guards from outside contractors; however, they do not train these people, who change all the time, in the proper procedures for emergencies. The security guards in many cases are the first to call the fire department and ambulances. They need an understanding of the plant's layout and the dangerous chemicals stored at the facility and up-to-date emergency contact names and telephone numbers.

The organization needs to test its plans for emergencies periodically, from fire drills to spill response and first aid. A review of the emergency plans needs to be done on a regular basis, especially when there are process changes, new construction, or changes that take place at an organization or after an emergency has taken place, so that plans can be revised and tested with a follow-up of communication and training.

Contractors and visitors need to know how to respond when there is an emergency within your organization. What training and communications do you have in place? In your emergency plan have a written process of evacuating your workplace, as well as the roles and responsibilities and internal and external lines of communication. Make sure that emergency equipment is available for use and is maintained in good working order.

As part of your emergency preparedness planning you will also need to plan on bringing business back to normal, with recovery of documentation and communications. What would your plan of action be?

In many emergency plans, sometimes we overlook the obvious—for instance, when preparing for emergencies at a zoo, we look at the people but may forget the emergency plan for removing the animals when a fire or flood takes place. Having an outside set of eyes on your management system helps to review what some would consider to be the norm.

It is important to review and, where necessary, revise your emergency preparedness plan, in particular after testing or after the occurrence of emergency situations.

Assess & Reflect #31

EMERGENCY PREPAREDNESS

Focus: Health and Safety—Prevention of Injury and Ill Health

❶ Has your organization *maintained* its emergency prevention, preparedness, and response program?
   a. Have you had any recent emergencies? What were they?
   b. Define what was done to plan for similar emergency situations.
   c. Was contact made with applicable government bodies?
   d. What impact has this emergency had on your organization?
   e. What changes happened due to this emergency (procedures, training, communications, process changes, design changes)?

❷ The last time you visited your branch office, were you provided with any information about emergency response at the site?

❸ Who is the lead emergency coordinator? Who is the company's spokesperson with the media, government? Do you have an emergency chain of command? Do you have backup personnel in the chain of command? Can you rely on these people during a crisis? Does your emergency team include the personnel responsible for the identification of hazards (risks) at your facility?

❹ Does your facility maintain a good relationship with local fire departments and local government services? In the event of an emergency, it is essential to have a good relationship with them.

❺ What backup plans does the company have in place? Loss of a key individual can also be a loss of data and information.

❻ What information does your company need in order to continue after the emergency is over? In some cases a facility may not be directly impacted; however, the emergency may prevent your workers from accessing the facility for weeks or even months. What would your backup system be for an off-site location?

7 What is the emergency number you would call on a mobile phone? Can you send text messages to these numbers? How? 112, 999, 911?

8 What are the evacuation time limits for your site(s)?

9 What sites does the company own that are in tornado zones? How are you prepared for such emergencies?

10 Does the facility(s) have a listing of inventory of hazardous materials? Where they are located?

11 Do you have security guards at your facility? Do they have current contacts for emergencies, up to date floor plans, current emergency preparedness plans?

12 Have you had an emergency drill at your location that included visitors, contractors? How was your drill? What do you measure for effectiveness of emergency preparedness?

Act

EMERGENCY PREPAREDNESS

FOCUS: PREVENTION OF INJURY AND ILL HEALTH

_____

_____

_____

_____

_____

_____

_____

_____

_____

_____

_____

_____

_____

_____

_____

_____

_____

_____

_____

_____

_____

_____

_____

_____

_____

_____

Notes

1. Occupational Safety & Health Administration. Available at www.OSHA.gov.

2. Health and Safety Executive. Available at www.hse.gov.uk.

3. Employment and Social Development Canada. Available at www4 .hrsdc.gc.ca/.3ndic.1t.4r@-eng.jsp?iid=20.

4. The document is available at www.ilo.org/publns.

5. GKN website (www.gkn.com/corporateresponsibility/Pages/health -and-safety.aspx) indicated that it had 92 sites registered to OHSAS 18001 and the remaining sites are working toward it.

6. "Walmart Statement by Jay Jorgensen Regarding the Bangladesh Worker Safety Initiative," July 10, 2013. Available from www.news .walmart.com.

7. "Wal-Mart signs corporate-wide settlement with US Labor De-partment. Available at https://www.osha.gov/pls/oshaweb/owadisp .show_document?p_table=NEWS_RELEASES&p_id=24495; or www.dol.gov.

CHAPTER 9

Integrated Principles for a Sustainable Business Management System

L ooking at business challenges and opportunities for the future is not an easy task. After reviewing the international standard principles for quality and then researching major corporations as to what they were working toward in environment and occupational health and safety, I present a list of key principles for business management to drive business success.

1. Business focus

The principles for business success need to be integrated to provide a management framework for all organizations to position themselves as innovators and leaders in integrating sustainability and long-term value into the management of their business operations for business growth and success.

When there is a like-minded framework followed by all businesses that includes quality, environment, health and safety, and

INTEGRATED PRINCIPLES

Business Management System Principles

1. Business focus
   a. Quality: Customer Satisfaction (Quality of processes, products and services)
   b. Environment: Prevention of pollution
   c. Occupational Health and Safety: Prevention of injury and ill health
   d. Financials
2. Leadership
3. Compliance with legal and other requirements
4. Involvement of people—innovation, participation, consultation, partnerships, and collaboration
5. Process approach—system approach to management
6. Management of resources—mutually beneficial supplier relationships
7. Operational control
8. Emergency preparedness
9. Performance evaluation
10. Factual approach to decision making and information sharing
11. Continual improvement

financials in managing a business, this will not only improve the sustainability of the individual company's business but also contribute to improving global sustainability. Companies will be managing the risks that apply to them and impacting others. They will be analyzing data, creating infrastructure in anticipation of added revenue, and rewarding results that improve business operations. The integrated management system to international standards provides a framework for effective and efficient business process management.

a. Quality—customer satisfaction

Organizations depend on their customers and therefore should understand current and future customer needs, meet customer requirements, and strive to exceed customer expectations.

Customer satisfaction is dependent upon meeting business needs and the agreed-upon level of quality to be achieved to benefit its operations. It may also require added value, improved business function, and performance. The supplier is to deliver products and/or services within the agreed cost plan and time to satisfy the customer requirements. The determination of this "success" requires a "quality" approach to management and an understanding of the level of risks.

b. Environment—prevention of pollution

Top management recognizes the priority of environmental management as an integral part of its business success, social responsibility, and sustainability. It leads by establishing vision, policy, objectives, programs, and practices to ensure its commitment to prevention of pollution and to ensure that environmental performance is integrated in the way they do business, throughout the organization.

c. Occupational health and safety—prevention of injury and ill health

Top management recognizes the priority of occupational health and safety management as an integral part of its business success. It leads by establishing vision, policy, objectives, programs, and practices to ensure its commitment to prevention of injury and ill health by controlling its risks and improving its OH&S performance.

d. Financials

Top management recognizes the priority of remaining focused on its business mission for growth, building a brand, and always managing to the bottom line (cash flow), for performance, productivity, and profits.

2. Leadership

Leaders are engaged and establish unity of purpose and direction for the organization. They create and maintain the internal environment in which people can become fully involved in achieving the organization's commitments and objectives. These objectives are prioritized and directed to the sustainability, innovation, creativity, and recognition of employees for the success of the organization and the management of its quality (customer satisfaction), environment (prevention of pollution), health and safety (prevention of injury and ill health), and financial needs (profitability) shaping future systems and contributing to society.

3. **Compliance with legal and other requirements**

    A commitment to comply with applicable legislation, regulations, guidelines, and policies (quality, environment, health and safety, business) is a permanent objective of the organization to ensure adequate systems, practices, and controls are in place.

4. **Involvement of people—innovation, participation, consultation, partnerships, and collaboration**

    People at all levels are the essence of an organization, and their full involvement enables their abilities to be used for the organization's benefit. Seek and engage internal/external advice, assistance, or strategic alliances and social networks where needed. Ensure talent management.

5. **Process approach**

    A desired result is achieved more efficiently when activities and related resources are managed as a process.

    a. **System approach to management**

        Identifying, understanding, and managing integrated and interrelated processes and their risks as a system contribute to the organization's effectiveness and efficiency in achieving its objectives.

6. **Management of resources**

    Top management ensures adequate and effective management of our resources—land (natural resources), labor (human resources—labor, training, competence, succession planning, communication/participation/consultation, specialized skills, organizational infrastructure), documentation, capital (financial resources), and technology (automation).

a. Mutually beneficial supplier relationship

An organization and its suppliers are interdependent, and a mutually beneficial relationship enhances the ability of both to create value.

7. Operational control

Establish, implement, monitor, measure, and maintain with risk management, change management, control of functions, activities, and processes associated with our risks (quality, environment, health and safety, financials).

8. Emergency preparedness

The organization is responsible for ensuring that it is prepared for and can respond to emergency situations and accidents and prevent or mitigate associated adverse environmental impacts and occupational health and safety consequences.

9. Performance evaluation

Monitoring and measurement of risks, plans, practices, and performance indicators form the basis for continual improvement. External unattached assessment, as well as internal, will identify business improvement opportunities and shortcomings and provide unbiased intelligence.

10. Factual approach to decision making and information sharing

Effective decisions are based on the analysis of correct data and information. Information sharing with authenticity and transparency builds trust and is made available to stakeholders.

11. Continual improvement

Continual improvement of the organization's overall performance should be a permanent objective of the organization for business sustainability, growth, and success. Senior management's main leadership tasks are to forecast and assess challenges and opportunities to be a positive force in the company and to society. To support advocacy and collaborative solutions, innovation, automation, and technology for ongoing continual improvement in overall performance, and making a difference.

PART III

Integrated Management System Implementation: Three Steps

Plan, Do, Check, Act—Deming

International standards adopted the four-step management method used in business for the control and continuous improvement of processes and products, the "Plan, Do, Check, Act" (PDCA) cycle, developed by the father of quality control, Dr. W. Edwards Deming. This cycle is ongoing, with each cycle improving and getting closer to the ultimate goal(s) of the organization.

Three-Step Process: Identify, Insure, Improve – Pilot

Improvement is a key factor in the success of any business in today's world. In 1994, Pilot Performance Resources Management Inc. formulated the Three Step Process: Identify, Insure, Improve, to give companies a simple process to implement and audit their management system framework according to international standards, which are provided through training, our consulting practice, and my ISO 9001 implementation guidebook.

The focus of a management system structure needs to be on "change" and "innovation" in order to "improve." I found that the PDCA cycle's wording, which came from the 1940s, did not emphasize this. Therefore I set in place these three steps, which major corporations and institutions in North America have followed, as outlined in my guidebook, *ISO 9001*, on how to implement and integrate a quality management system with environment and health and safety. These three steps have been followed by over 2,000 major corporations and institutions in North America.

These simple steps can be applied to every process while keeping it simple, but focusing on "continual improvement" of each process.

Step One   You **"Identify"** the process(es), its risks, planning of objectives and strategic measurable plans for each process, and requirements and resources tied to the process.

Step Two   Then you **"Insure"** the provision of support systems—resources, documentation, training, communication for operational control of the business processes.

Step Three   The **"Improve"** looks at the monitoring, measuring, analysis, and evaluation—audits, nonconformance, corrective action, and management reviews of each process.

Why? Because all eyes (*Is*) are watching you (see Figure P3.1).

Management System Implementation

I've asked this question of many CEOs and managers: "To what criteria do you manage your business?" The answers come back like this: "We manage our business to our own corporate requirements; we don't have to follow anyone's criteria; we build our own." However, when they try to explain what that structure is, they cannot.

Challenges are before us in business. It is important to look to your business management system and put in place systems thinking that will be understood by others doing business with you, whether it is in your community, country, or the world.

FIGURE P3.1

Pilot's Three-Step Process for Implementing Management Systems Meeting ISO Standards

The Eyes are Watching Us in
Enviroment, Health and Safety, and Quality

Step One: Identify. The eyes are looking up, "Oh, my, what a task I have before me!"

Step Two: Insure. The eyes are crossed, dealing with all the documents, data, details.

Step Three: Improve. The eyes are focused on going forward with continual improvement.

Source: "Three-Step System Approach to Change Management," by Jayne Pilot, ISOFocus publication.

Structures need to be in place that will encourage and support the business practices and success of your organization, supporting innovation and automation. It is key that document management is managed for the analysis of data, keeping in mind the value for not only the organization but also the customer. Management system structures need to be understood by not only the organization but also its suppliers, customers, and all its stakeholders.

Assess & Reflect #32

ACCORDING TO WHAT CRITERIA DO I MANAGE OUR BUSINESS?

_____

_____

_____

_____

_____

_____

_____

_____

_____

_____

_____

_____

_____

_____

_____

_____

_____

_____

_____

_____

_____

_____

_____

CHAPTER 10

International Management Systems

An effective manager knows the importance of having business principles in place to focus the organization on the vision for its business success.

How do you manage your business, and what management system framework do you use?

Leaders are looking to improve business operations to access timely data and information to make informed opportune decisions while working in the global competitive marketplace. CEOs and top management not only need to understand what the financial bottom line expectations are but also require information on operations that support getting to the end result. They need to know what processes or systems are in place to support success in business effectiveness and efficiency.

The International Organization for Standardization (ISO), based in Geneva, Switzerland, is a worldwide federation of national standards bodies from over 190 countries and has been working for the last 60 plus years in developing standards to facilitate international commerce.[1] Standards have been developed by international technical committees, made up of experts in the subject, with input from relevant others, such as major organizations, governments, and nongovernmental bodies from around the world. These standards set a framework for the successful operation of a business, ensuring continual improvement and the success of the business.

The three key international management system standards are ISO 9001 for quality, ISO 14001 for environment, and OHSAS 18001 for occupational health and safety. Management systems provide the framework to manage ongoing identification of the organization's requirements and risks, and to put in place strategic measureable planning, implementation, control, monitoring, measurement, and continual improvement of one's business operations, with the ability to respond to customer's needs quickly and manage risks.

Using the framework of management systems that meet international standards has assisted many organizations around the world in improving market competitiveness, effectiveness of operations, increasing productivity and greater profitability, and breaking down barriers to international trade.

North America Lags Behind

Since 1993, ISO Central Secretariat has outsourced the collection and compilation of a yearly survey that outlines the worldwide certification of management systems. The 2013 survey gave results for 2012 and is posted on its website (www.iso.org/iso/news). These figures don't include organizations that have implemented ISO as their framework but have chosen not to seek certification. The report includes a breakdown of certificates by industry sector, as well as world, region, and country, and can be purchased from ISO.

By the end of December 2012, there were 1,101,272 Quality Management (ISO 9001) certificates issued in 184 countries. This steady growth in quality management system implementation around the world confirms the importance of ISO 9001 for global supply chains.

The top 10 countries leading in quality management certification in 2012, in order, are: China, Italy, Spain, Germany, Japan, United Kingdom, France, India, United States, and Brazil. The top countries for growth in the number of certificates in 2012 were Spain, China, Romania, France,

Germany, Portugal, Argentina, Indonesia, Switzerland, and Vietnam. The 2012 totals represent an increase of 2 percent (21,625) over the 2011 numbers.

North America lags behind, with the fewest ISO 9001 certificates, with only the following attained in 2012: United States, 26,177; Canada, 6,907; Mexico, 5,502. What will this do for global trade for North America in the future?

The top five industrial sectors for ISO 9001 certificates in 2012 were in the following areas: basic metal and fabricated metal products; construction, electrical, and optical equipment; wholesale and retail trade; repairs of motor vehicles, motorcycles, and personal and household goods; and machinery and equipment.

We do know that many of the manufacturing industries have moved to China and India and that many of the corporate offices are in North America. Will North America be a service industry? North America is well known for its policies, know-how, and technology, which are sought after around the world. Government bodies and businesses have been involved with the development of standards and policies in North America and have given this information away free to other countries.

When I researched the countries who lead in certification, I found that these countries provided support to their small and medium-sized businesses to implement management systems with funding and tax incentive programs. When I approached the Canadian government for such programs, it said it is working to provide jobs in Canada. Without supporting business principles and practices meeting international requirements, it will be very difficult to ensure jobs for the future.

ISO 14001 (environmental management systems) had 285,844 certificates, a growth of 9 percent (+23,887) in 167 countries, with the top three countries being China, Japan, and Italy. The highest growth in certificates was in China, Spain, and Italy. Although many of the environmental technologies are in North America, the certification is not.

The ISO survey does not include OHSAS 18001 (occupational health and safety) as it is not an ISO standard but a British standard.

China is in the top 10 countries for six out of the seven standards that were covered by the survey, a definite leader in ISO 9001, ISO 14001, ISO 22000, and ISO/TS 16949 (automotive). It is interesting to note that Japan takes the lead in the information security sector (ISO 27001), with about 35 percent of certificates. IT is definitely important to Japan; I hope other countries are paying attention.

Having trained organizations from manufacturers to service providers to institutions since 1994 on how to implement international standards and conduct audits, I am amazed that participants have not included owners, presidents, CEOs, or directors of a company, but middle managers and ISO coordinators. The business structure and changes to an organization need to start with top management. For those organizations that are considering putting in a management system structure meeting ISO standards or that presently have ISO standards in place, it is important for owners and top management to understand what the structure consists of, how it can assist in providing correct information to make decisions, and the systems in place for tracking and improving business operations.

Many organizations have put in systems only for marketing reasons and do not understand or utilize the dynamics of the ISO management system framework for their business operations and improving profitability.

Business Benefits: Business Structure for Success

International standards provide a framework for management systems, to assist leaders in driving business success. They facilitate continual improvement in business operations, providing a framework to provide what I call the three Ps: performance, productivity, and profits.

The ISO process-based framework assures others that you have identified and understood customer requirements and have **consistently** implemented processes and procedures in place to ensure effective and efficient operation of your business to provide customer satisfaction. As well, your management system framework supports innovation, change management, automation, and technology.

It starts with your identification of your business processes and requirements for customer and legal issues, understanding your business risks tied to these areas to properly manage them through allocation of resources and operational controls. Strategic planning is done by setting clear measurable objectives, concentrating on customer satisfaction and partnerships that will create growth, and ensuring that these are understood and supported throughout the organization. Operational controls are put in place for product or service realization and support processes have been identified.

The following processes will support reviews for increases in profitability: performance evaluation, monitoring and measurement of planning, and use of resources and improving processes. Verification of management system effectiveness and efficiency and continual improvement are supported through the internal and external audit process, helping organizations clearly identify where they are going astray and which areas need further improvement.

Access to World Trade—Global Marketplace

ISO standards are adopted by many governments around the world to ensure that requirements are the same for import and export, facilitating transportation of goods and services from one country to another. Standards help organizations to compete on a level playing field. Doing business globally requires a company to show to others around the world that they have systems in place to manage their business success. ISO's management system standards are supported by over 190 countries.

Reduced Risks

A management system meeting international standards puts in place controls to manage a company's products or services, insuring that it is consistent with not only customer and regulatory requirements but also its own operational controls and strategic plans. Not only does it assist in identifying one's own company risks, but also it improves global management of climate change and energy and environmental issues tied to air, water, and soil quality, which impact us all.

Social Responsibility, Credibility, Competitive Advantage

Today many products and services from around the world are purchased by consumers who want them to be safe for consumption or for use by children and adults alike and to be of excellent quality.

Companies want to do business with other companies who are credible and value the welfare of society and our environment, which means being green and supporting corporate social responsibility to make a positive impact on society while doing business. International case studies are found on the ISO website.[2]

Improved Operational Controls

The focus of management systems to ISO standards is on continual improvement of the whole management system.

The operational controls concentrate on the product/service realization day-to-day measures that are tied to production, supported by standing operating procedures and delivered according to a set of requirements for the customer. It is within operational control that quality control is managed and the supporting processes for purchasing, inventory, and logistics come into play to support production and/or service. It is here where nonproductive and nonconforming product costs, such as scrap, rework, warranty claims, late delivery, and nonconforming products, can make a company unsustainable.

A quality management system helps your organization identify its operational processes, quality controls, risks, and objectives, staying focused on meeting not only customer and legal requirements but also your own, and improving processes, thus reducing operational costs and improving your bottom line.

This chapter looked at some of the challenges for business in the near future and the principles for managing business successfully. One of the major challenges will be to have systems in place prior to the loss of key managers due to the grey tsunami, to capture their knowledge and know-how. Management system structures are the framework that will secure the information and data related to your processes and legal requirements before they go out the door.

Assess, Reflect, Act: Driving Sustainability to Business Success

The Assess, Reflect, Act section after each principle tied to quality, environment, and occupational health and safety was developed to help you as top management use critical thinking to drive business success. It provides an opportunity to gather information about the principles you have in place, so you can remain focused on fulfilling your business mission and meeting challenges of today.

I then introduced you to the benefits of international standards. In Part III, you have the opportunity to assess where your weak link(s) are in your management system, so that your business is built on a solid framework that ensures your business success.

Notes

1. International Organization for Standardization (ISO), www.iso.org.
2. For further supporting information on benefits, refer to international case studies on the ISO website at www.iso.org: "10 Good Things ISO Standards Do for SMEs," "Global Solutions for CEOs," and "Economic Benefits of Standards." You may view full reports and presentations from such organizations as PT Wika Beton, NTUC Fairprice, and Siemens AG.

CHAPTER 11

Management Systems

Business Plans vs. Management Systems Meeting ISO Standards

As a manager, you have always been taught to have a business plan. Outlined ahead is the structure of both a business plan and a business management system so you can quickly see the difference between the two.

As a member of the plenary group in Canada to bring auditor certification to the country, initiated by the Chartered Accountants of Canada, I brought to the attention of the banks the need to make the business plan structure more like the management system structure, so that companies would sustain their businesses for the long term.

The first component that is missing in the business plan is the process approach, which requires the business owner to identify the interconnection of its business processes.

The emphasis in the business plan is on "planning," not on the sustainability of the business management system. A management system structure requires the organization to identify its risks tied to its processes in its planning stages, and then to put in place support systems and controls. The emphasis in a management system is on continual improvement of running the business by monitoring and measuring operations and ensuring data

FIGURE 11.1

Business Plans or Management System Approach

Business Plan/Policy Structure	Management System Criteria—ISO
Formal statement of a set of business goals and plans for reaching those goals.	**MS—Process approach:** develop, implement, improve effectiveness of management system processes—**ongoing control**
Background information about the organization or team attempting to reach those goals.	**Planning:** support business principle. Identifying risks (quality, environment, health and safety). Develop & implement policy, objectives, targets, legal, customer requirements
Sales and Marketing Plan	**Insure implementation:** marketing, supply chain, operations, documentation/records, communications, training, and so forth
Operating and Human Resources Plan	**Monitor and measure:** operational controls, objectives & targets, compliance
Action Plan	**Internal and third-party audits, management review**

Source: Pilot Performance Resource Management Inc.

analysis and performance evaluation through internal and third-party audits. This is a key area that is missing in the business plan (see Figure 11.1).

Regardless of the size of an organization, the goods or services, or the sector, systems thinking is important for the effectiveness and efficiency of business operations.

Where Is the Weak Link in Your Management System?

Figure 11.2 shows you the key process areas for an organization: (1) its leadership and planning of its business processes, (2) processes for the implementation of the business, and (3) the operational controls and monitoring and measurement analysis for the improvement of the processes. Understanding the risks tied to each of these areas and the weak links associated with the process helps the organization manage and grow the business with strength.

FIGURE 11.2

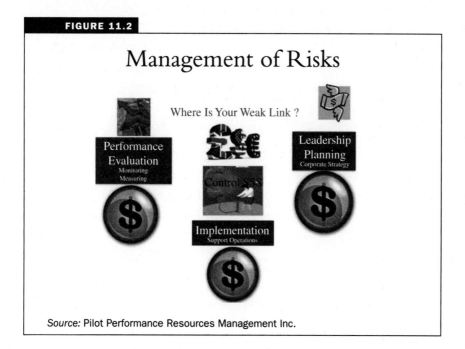

Management of Risks

Where Is Your Weak Link ?

Performance Evaluation
Monitoring Measuring

Leadership Planning
Corporate Strategy

Controls

Implementation
Support Operations

Source: Pilot Performance Resources Management Inc.

Why Use Management Systems Meeting International Standards?

In the global economy, it is crucial to understand how your suppliers and customers manage their business operations, as many of the business systems are interconnected. Companies are no longer just next door to develop close relationships with. Companies like to deal with other businesses that have a structure in place that they understand and work to.

Business relationships are crucial, and decision makers need to feel confident that the organization they are working with has identified its risks and has structures in place to monitor and measure processes before problems occur. These may be related to the following, which could have an impact on their business: on-time delivery, nonconforming products or services, compliance or legal issues that will stop the operation of the company or have an impact on their products, and customer satisfaction.

The global business market requires a corporate strategy, not with a business plan but a management system. Using systems thinking at the point of customer contact with quality control, and at the point of operations with risk identification, ensures that controls are in place, with monitoring, measurement, analysis, and evaluation.

Management systems meeting international standards are a closed-loop system for ongoing planning, implementing, monitoring, measuring, and evaluating continual improvement of business operations. The ISO standards provide a recognized structure that is understood and recognized around the world as facilitating international commerce, and they are accepted by over 190 countries.

These management systems have been researched with input from top corporations around the world, through ISO Technical Committees, outlining a framework that ensures effectiveness and efficiency with continual improvement being at the forefront for business success.

When an organization has compliance issues and goes to court, the judges in many cases have required companies to implement management systems to international standards for environment and health and safety, therefore an ISO management system is a defense for due diligence.

Three Main ISO Management Systems

The three main management systems that many organizations implement are: quality (ISO 9001), environment (ISO 14001), and health and safety (OHSAS 18001), as they apply to all organizations. As outlined in Figure 11.3, there are many other management systems, such as energy (ISO 50001), which could, as an example, be integrated with the environment (ISO 14001) standard. The basis for many other industry standards, such as food safety (ISO 22000), is the ISO 9001. All management system standards utilize the ISO 19011 Guideline for auditing.

The quality management system (QM) ISO 9001's focus is on ensuring "customer satisfaction," providing products or services that consistently meet customer and applicable legal requirements. Customers know that when you have a QMS in place your organization has

FIGURE 11.3

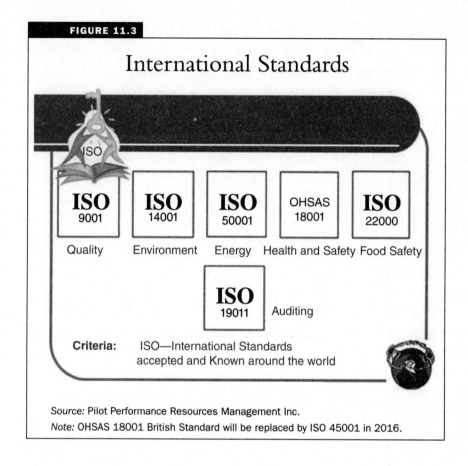

International Standards

ISO 9001	ISO 14001	ISO 50001	OHSAS 18001	ISO 22000
Quality	Environment	Energy	Health and Safety	Food Safety

ISO 19011 — Auditing

Criteria: ISO—International Standards accepted and Known around the world

Source: Pilot Performance Resources Management Inc.
Note: OHSAS 18001 British Standard will be replaced by ISO 45001 in 2016.

identified its requirements, as well as legal needs, and has a structure in place to manage and control the quality of the product/service it will deliver.

Global Registration Results

ISO contracts out a survey, which outlines the previous year's management system registrations around the world.

The majority of the registrations in 2012 were: Europe at 43.1 percent and Asia at 43.1 percent, with only 3.5 percent in North America. Central and South America had 4.7 percent.

North America is the lowest. Why is this happening? What does North America have to learn from this? Are we losing our business opportunities? Organizations use the ISO certification system for competitive advantage showing quality performance to their customers, whether they have it in place or not. Has your government supported business to put in structures like China and India have, providing tax incentive programs?

Supply-chain risk will be crucial for global business. Information on suppliers may be difficult to attain, however when you have an ISO 9001 certification in place, it will show that you as a supplier can provide quality products/service with confidence, mitigate risk, and build lasting business partnerships. The certification assists in identifying high-quality suppliers and low-quality ones in the global marketplace.

Management System Framework—Generic

More and more organizations are integrating their management systems and, as a result, the framework for management systems needs to be standardized. ISO/TMB (Technical Management Board) produced the Annex SL (previously known as ISO Guide 83) in 2012 to help deliver consistent and compatible management system standards.

This generic management system framework will help eliminate duplications and confusions when integrating and certifying management systems, as they will all become consistent and, hopefully, use the same definitions.

All new or next-revision ISO management systems will be required to adhere to this generic management system framework within the next few years.

Standards are usually reviewed and revised every five years to keep them relevant and reflect changes in business requirements.

ISO management standards will, however, require additional discipline-specific requirements for management systems operations, which will be addressed in the upcoming revisions, such as quality, environment, energy, occupational health and safety, food safety, and information security. The Annex SL does not apply to ISO 19011, which is the Guideline for Auditing Management Systems.

The new quality management standard, ISO 9001:2015, is following this structure. This will impact companies that have their management systems in place meeting the previous revision, ISO 9001:2008, as they will need to align their management systems to this new structure and amend their organizations' manuals. It is expected that a three-year grace period will be given.

I have in the past ten plus years encouraged companies registered for quality management systems to look in to integrating their management system to include environment and health and safety. Zochem, Canada's largest zinc oxide manufacturer and a client of mine, received the first registration in North America by BSI in 2003 for an integrated management system.

Management System Standardization—Annex SL

The Annex SL brings the following major clause numbers and titles to all management systems and the need to be identical and easy to integrate. The main sections of your management system will include the following, and content for the specific standard that will be added (environment, health and safety, etc.). The revised standards will follow this outline, starting with the revised ISO 9001:2015 Quality management system.

1. Scope
2. Normative References
3. Terms and Definitions
4. Context of the Organization
5. Leadership
6. Planning
7. Support
8. Operation
9. Performance Evaluation
10. Improvement

Detailed Content in Management System Clauses

4. Context of the Organization
   4.1 Understanding Organization and Its Context
   4.2 Understanding Needs and Expectations of Interested Parties

Integrated Management Systems

Many organizations operate their businesses in "silos," duplicating functions rather than harmonizing and directing all parts of the organization in an integrated management system approach.

Document management can be costly. The cost of producing a single document can reach $250 or more, depending on the number of people involved in its development and approval, not to mention the costs associated with copying, filing, and retrieving documents (costs can exceed $120 for misfiled documents). Filing electronically does help but only if you know the right keywords or file names.

An integrated management system is a framework that integrates the management of your business processes so that they function together, aligning their direction with common goals to improve process operations and, ultimately, the performance of the whole organization. By having an integrated management system you will eliminate redundancies, documentation, conflicting and duplicated procedures, and the chance of conflict with responsibilities and relationships, and gain the ability to create harmonizing and optimizing business practices and prioritize the plans for the company. This will also result in improving communication and facilitating training, competence, and employee development.

The ISO standards ensure the monitoring and control of your processes, which are supported by verification of your management system through audits, both internal and external.

An organization may wish to integrate two or more management systems. Examples of typical management systems that can be integrated include: ISO 9001 (quality), ISO 14001 (environmental management), ISO 50001 (energy), OHSAS 18001 (occupational health and safety), ISO/IEC 27001 (information security), ISO/IEC 2000 (IT service management), ISO 22000 (food safety), and BSI ISO 22301 (business continuity management).

The framework for integration starts with a quality management system (ISO 9001) as the baseline, identifying one's business processes. This standard ensures that goods and services (previously referred to as products or services) consistently meet customers' requirements and that quality is improving. This standard, as outlined in the previous chapters, is based on a number of quality management principles and the process approach.

Organizations that have a mature quality management system would find it easy to introduce environment and health and safety to their ISO 9001 structure, as they have already identified their processes and process flow, addressing quality risks, and they now can address the risks tied to environment and health and safety. Addressing each process can also include addressing and prioritizing the objectives tied to the process.

The implementation and operation's processes have required a manual; however, the new ISO 9001:2015 is getting away from documentation, as many organizations have computerized systems in place and online structures.

Integrated Management System Standard—PAS 99:2006

The British Standards Institute (BSI) in partnership with BSI Management Systems developed the first specification that accommodated the interest in an integrated approach to management systems and governance of organizational risk, called "PAS 99:2006—Specification of Common Management System Requirements as a Framework for Integration." Should an organization wish to apply for registration for PAS 99, you would be required to demonstrate that there is *one* management system that encompasses all existing management systems standards.

An organization does not necessarily need to have its integrated management system registered to the British Standard PAS 99. Your organization can have its integrated management system registered for all three standards—ISO 9001, 14001, and OHSAS 18001—but audited all at the same time with three certificates provided. Check with your registration body to see if it accepts registration for PAS 99, as many registrars are authorized for certification for the individual standards: ISO 9001, ISO 14001, and OHSAS 18001. With the revised ISO standards following the Annex SL, integration will be easier to implement.

CHAPTER 12

Step One: Identify

Understanding the Organization

What is the purpose of your organization? To serve your customers.

The first section of this book gave you as a leader an opportunity to Assess-Reflect-Act on principles relevant to your organization. The questions we as managers ask ourselves or others helps us determine where we are in our organization and where we need to be.

Five Most Important Questions

Peter Ferdinand Drucker, an Austrian-born American management consultant, educator, and author of 40 books and thousands of articles, was a leader in management education and invented the concept known as "management by objectives." He was well known in Japan, where he was considered similar to W. Edwards Deming, the quality guru.

Drucker's writings state that a company's primary responsibility is to serve its customers. Profit is not the primary goal, but rather an essential condition for the company's continued existence. He was a consultant to senior executives for more than 50 years.

Readers may be interested in Drucker's book called *The Five Most Important Questions You Will Ever Ask about Your Organization* (Wiley). Drucker's questions for the organization are:

1. What is our mission?

2. Who is our customer?

3. What does the customer value?

4. What are our results?

5. What is our plan?

This informative book will challenge readers to take a close look at the very heart of their organizations and what drives them. It is a tool for self-assessment and transformation.

Who Are Your Customers?

Today, for some companies, the customer may be their head office, rather than the actual end user. Drucker was a supporter of outsourcing, and today more and more companies are outsourcing work or have separate companies that do the manufacturing of products in other countries, and therefore they are not connected with the user. This makes it even more critical to understand not only the requirements for their customer, the head office, but also the requirements for the end users and what they value.

It is very important to understand who your customers are when doing business and to know which customers generate profits for you.

The Pareto principle, also known as the 80-20 rule, states that roughly 80 percent of the effects come from 20 percent of the causes. It is a common rule of thumb in business that only 20 percent of a company's customers contribute to profits and the remaining 80 percent generate losses. Of course the remaining 80 percent could be profitable in the future or provide knowledge or expertise that would be needed for future development.

Which of Your Customers Generate the 20 Percent?

Customer analysis is crucial in order to address market share. Understanding the needs of your customers and how your product/service satisfies their needs is the basis of your market and business plans. It used to be that price and quality were dominant factors for consumer purchases; however, today, business-to-business (B2B) transactions are also important, tied to delivery schedules and payment terms with purchases done on the Internet for convenience. Additionally, understanding what activities are driving customers' orders to be nonprofitable is important. Typical customer-related processes are: processing the sales order, billing, customer visits, engineering/design changes, packaging and handling (special requests), processing shipments, and customer satisfaction.

Assess & Reflect #33

WHICH CUSTOMERS GENERATE YOUR PROFITS?

The 20 percent rule: It is a common rule of thumb in business that only 20 percent of a company's customers contribute to profits.

Name them:

_____

_____

_____

_____

_____

_____

_____

_____

_____

_____

_____

_____

_____

_____

_____

_____

_____

_____

_____

_____

_____

_____

_____

Management System Planning

This section gives you an overview of the tasks required in implementing an integrated management system framework.

1. Identify "Scope" of the Integrated Management System (IMS).

When we look at business management systems we need to consider their boundaries or scope, the composition of the processes involved, the inputs and outputs of these processes, and the specialized elements that perform specialized quality control, environmental, and health and safety functions.

The scope of an IMS is what's printed on an organization's accredited ISO certificate, which describes its boundaries and is included in the IMS manual.

  a. Is your management system for the whole organization or a part of it?

- Location—physical boundaries (listing addresses)
- Details of the goods and services offered
- Outline of main processes for goods/service realization

  b. Do you have exclusions (e.g., design and development)?

2. Determine the Need for Integration.

  a. What disciplines or standards will your management system include?

- ISO 9001, 14001, OHSAS 18001

  b. Gap analysis: Companies wishing to implement a management system meeting international standards should start by doing a gap analysis to find out what the organization has in place and what the gaps are, related to international standard requirements.

  c. What standard training requirements are needed?

  d. Who will coordinate the management system implementation? Will there be a team approach (members)?

3. Understand the Context of the Organization.

What commitments are you as a top manager making?

Refer back to Part I, where I talked about principles and presented questions for you to consider, as well as ones you could develop yourself under "Assess/Reflect" and "Act."

What is your focus for the organization?

a. Quality—customer satisfaction

b. Environment—prevention of pollution—in what areas?

c. Occupational health and safety—prevention of injury and ill health

d. Financial, etc.

e. Other

Set vision, mission, and values

a. Define business principles, vision, and mission to follow.

b. Communicate where your organization will be on a defined timeline.

4. Determine the Needs and Expectations of Interested Parties.

a. Customers

b. Marketplace

c. Shareholders

d. Employees

e. Contractors

f. Distributors/agents

g. Suppliers

h. Other:

Many organizations have seen their marketplaces dry up; understanding your marketplace is crucial to knowing when to change.

Determining the issues and requirements of interested parties can assist you in understanding the inputs to your management system.

Assess & Reflect #34

WHAT COMMITMENTS AM I MAKING?
WHAT IS OUR PURPOSE?
WHAT IS OUR VISION?
WHAT IS OUR MISSION?

_____

_____

_____

_____

_____

_____

_____

_____

_____

_____

_____

_____

_____

_____

_____

_____

_____

_____

_____

_____

_____

_____

Assess & Reflect #35

WHAT IS OUR FOCUS FOR THE ORGANIZATION?

1. Quality—customer satisfaction
2. Environment—prevention of pollution
3. Occupational health and safety—prevention of injury and ill health
4. Financial, etc.
5. Other: sustainability

_____

_____

_____

_____

_____

_____

_____

_____

_____

_____

_____

_____

_____

_____

_____

_____

_____

_____

_____

Leadership and Commitment

The ISO 9001:2015 revision for quality requires senior management to be more actively involved in the system. Leadership has an emphasis on hands-on involvement in the management system.

Ensure that the requirements of the management system are integrated into organization's business processes.

- Top management is accountable for the effectiveness of the management system.
- Demonstrate commitment by ensuring the MS achieves its outcomes.
- Set a clear measurable direction for the organization.
- Create a supportive environment—team members unafraid to move forward, to be innovative, to take risks, and to grow.
- Ensure all processes and applicable risks are identified and are controlled. Management of change—identify risks when reviewing potential consequence of the change.
- Commit to comply with applicable legal requirements.
- Provide adequate support systems and resources.
- Communicate the importance of the MS and requirements for participation in its effective implementation.
- Ensure monitoring, measurement, analysis, evaluation of data, internal audit, and management review of the MS.
- Choose verification through self-declaration or registration of the MS by third party.

Policy

Top management outlines the commitments it makes related to its intentions to conduct its business affairs and operations on a formal document. This statement guides the organization's employees, clients, the public, and other stakeholders on what the organization is committing to. The type of policy statement referred to in this book is one addressing the management system of the organization tied to quality, environment, and health and safety (see Business Management System Manual, Chapter 13 for an example). Policy statements are reviewed yearly to see that they are still applicable and, where required, make changes.

What are you as president/CEO/manager committing to?

1. Comply with management system and business requirements.
2. Continually improve your business.
3. Meet customer requirements and provide customer satisfaction.
4. Manage the following risks: Quality
   a. Prevent pollution
   b. Prevent injury and ill health—provide a safe environment
   c. Financial
   d. Other: social, political
5. Comply with applicable legal and other requirements (e.g., responsible care, industry codes of practice, union agreements).
6. What do you want the reader to know about your business (that you set goals and measurable objectives, have a management system that meets ISO (9001/14001) criteria, operate in a number of countries, etc.)?

Policy Statement Review

1. Does your policy statement outline who your company is? Are you the corporate office or a branch office? Where are you located? What does your business do?

   Many times policy statements are reviewed individually, and it is difficult to know if one applies to the corporate office or branch office. Does the reader know your company and what you do? How?

2. Is your policy statement dated? Is the date current? When was the last time you changed your policy statement?

3. Do employees or those working for your organization understand how your policy statement applies to the work that they do in the organization?

4. How do you communicate your policy statement? To whom? What interested parties? Is it available to the public? How?

Assess & Reflect #36

POLICY STATEMENT
WHAT AM I COMMITTED TO? VALUE?
WHAT DO READERS UNDERSTAND THAT OUR COMPANY VALUES FROM OUR POLICY STATEMENT?

_____

_____

_____

_____

_____

_____

_____

_____

_____

_____

_____

_____

_____

_____

_____

_____

_____

_____

_____

_____

_____

_____

_____

_____

_____

Process Approach

Integral to the business's direction and success is the identification of your processes in managing your business, their sequence, and their interaction.

A process approach requires the organization to identify the following and then determine the inputs and outputs for each process, its sequence, and its interaction, reviewing its risks and requirements.

Determine the following:

a. Management system processes (see Figure 12.1).

   Outsourced processes (external providers).

b. Process map of sequence (high-level); you can also do drilled-down process maps (see Figure 12.2).

   Review the inputs and outputs expected for each process.

c. Risks (quality, environment, health and safety) tied to each process for normal/abnormal/emergency, operational conditions, external provision of goods and services (outsourcing—if not already in place).

d. Comply with applicable legal and other requirements.

e. Customer satisfaction requirements.

f. Responsibilities and authorities for each process.

Risks

Ensure your managers have identified risks associated with process operations, tied to the bottom line (what, who, how, when, cost). Use a risk-based approach to determine the type and extent of controls that would be appropriate. A management system acts as a preventative tool addressing the risks (ensuring conformity of goods and services and customer satisfaction), as well as prevention or reduction of undesired effects and achievement of improvement or opportunities for improvement (OFI) to achieve its objectives.

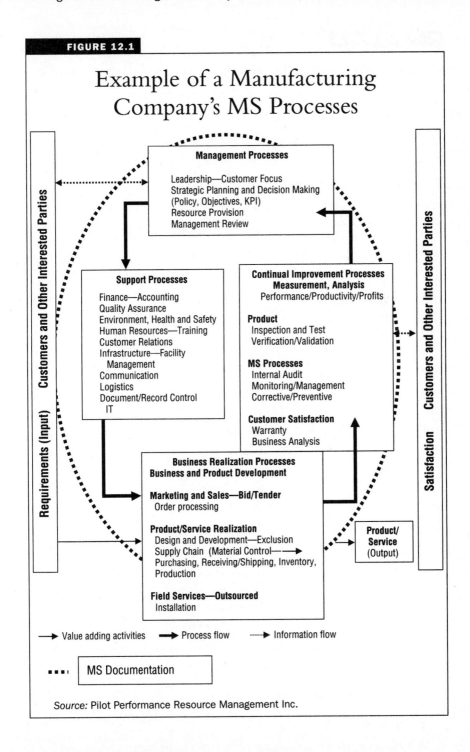

FIGURE 12.1

Example of a Manufacturing Company's MS Processes

Customers and Other Interested Parties

Requirements (Input)

Customers and Other Interested Parties

Satisfaction

Management Processes

Leadership—Customer Focus
Strategic Planning and Decision Making
(Policy, Objectives, KPI)
Resource Provision
Management Review

Support Processes

Finance—Accounting
Quality Assurance
Environment, Health and Safety
Human Resources—Training
Customer Relations
Infrastructure—Facility
  Management
Communication
Logistics
Document/Record Control
  IT

**Continual Improvement Processes
Measurement, Analysis**
Performance/Productivity/Profits

Product
Inspection and Test
Verification/Validation

MS Processes
Internal Audit
Monitoring/Management
Corrective/Preventive

Customer Satisfaction
Warranty
Business Analysis

**Business Realization Processes
Business and Product Development**

Marketing and Sales—Bid/Tender
Order processing

Product/Service Realization
Design and Development—Exclusion
Supply Chain (Material Control——▶
Purchasing, Receiving/Shipping, Inventory,
Production

Field Services—Outsourced
Installation

**Product/
Service**
(Output)

—▶ Value adding activities   ▬▶ Process flow   ┈┈▶ Information flow

▪▪▪▮   MS Documentation

Source: Pilot Performance Resource Management Inc.

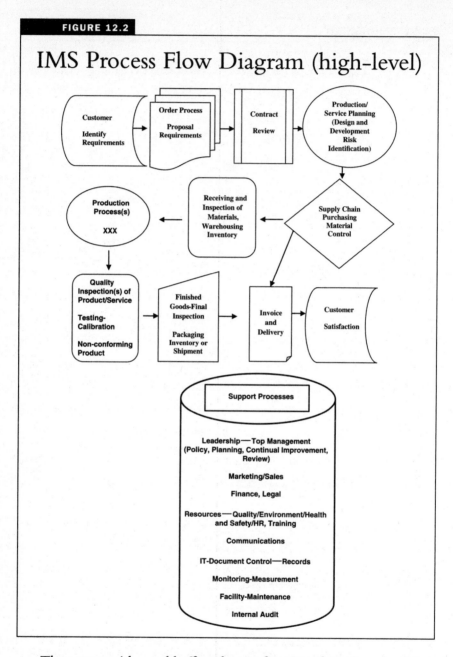

FIGURE 12.2

IMS Process Flow Diagram (high-level)

These seven risks could affect the conformity of goods and services as well as customer satisfaction and impact:

1. Financial

2. Quality—customer requirements and customer satisfaction

3. Environment—prevention of pollution

Consider: air emissions, waste generation (reuse/recycle, solid, electronic), hazardous materials, water/sanitary sewer, ground water, consumption of resources (water, energy, materials), contamination of land/soil, etc.

4. Health and safety—prevention of OH&S hazards

Consider hazard areas: chemical, biological, mechanical, physical, ergonomic, fire, and special (related to weather, earthquakes, confined spaces, etc.)

5. Social

6. Emergency preparedness

7. Change management

Employ management systems and procedures designed to prevent activities or conditions that pose a threat, to minimize risk, protect, and preserve.

Determine significance criteria used to determine risks, with legal being one factor and others being severity, frequency, and probability. This information needs to be reviewed in a team approach, with input from all levels to ensure process risks have been identified. This is an ongoing commitment for identification of risks, when new projects are developed, process or procedure changes occur, prior to implementing change.

When determining controls or considering changes to existing controls tied to occupational health and safety, the hierarchy outlined by OHSAS 18001 standard is excellent:

1. Elimination

2. Substitution

3. Engineering controls

4. Signage/warning and or administrative controls

5. Personal protective equipment

How are you as a leader letting others know that your company has identified its risks?

Risk Resources

ISO 31000:2009 Risk Management—Principles and Guidelines (US adoption ANSI/ASSE Z690.2-2011), (CAN/CSA ISO 31000)

IEC 31010:2009 Risk Assessment Techniques (US adoption ANSI/ASSE Z690.3-2011)

ISO Guide 73:2009 Vocabulary for Risk Management (US adoption ANSI/ASSE Z690.1-2011)

Global Citizenship—Western Digital's Commitment

Western Digital's president and CEO, Stephen Milligan, has done just this by outlining in a letter on the company's website its commitment to "global citizenship." Its policy statement is not the only document posted. It has informed the world of its commitments to protecting and preserving our environment, health, and safety, and of its global citizenship and how it is doing it.

As I read further on its website I saw that its management systems met ISO 9001, ISO 14001, and OHSAS 18001. It is living their management system structure according to international standards.[1]

Assess & Reflect #37

WHAT ARE OUR # 1 RISKS?

1 Quality—customer satisfaction
2 Environment—prevention of pollution
3 Occupational health and safety—prevention of injury and ill health
4 Financial, etc.
5 Other

_____

_____

_____

_____

_____

_____

_____

_____

_____

_____

_____

_____

_____

_____

_____

_____

_____

_____

_____

_____

_____

_____

_____

_____

Legal Commitment—Compliance

As a leader of your organization you have the responsibility of ensuring that you are following and meeting applicable legal and other requirements. You must demonstrate a commitment to complying with applicable laws and regulations, which you outlined in your policy statement. Understanding these requirements can keep you as a manager out of jail or prevent the paying of huge fines if not in compliance.

Programs and procedures need to be put in place that are tied to responsibilities, in order to ensure compliance.

1. Identify what legal and other requirements are applicable.

   Do you as a manager have an understanding of your legal requirements? This is usually managed by someone else in your organization, however as a CEO, do you have a copy of this legal listing and the associated tasks?

2. What are the associated applicable tasks?

3. Who is responsible for legal activities (reporting to corporate, reporting to shareholders, government, media, etc., providing appropriate training to employees and contractors)?

   Do they keep you updated on the status of compliance issues? How?

4. Compliance is an ongoing objective of the company. Include it in the change management process.

5. Communication log on compliance activities.

6. Monitoring and measurement of operations—various parameters to maintain legal compliance (environment, health and safety, quality). Who is responsible? Do they report on maintenance of these requirements to you?

7. Compliance review or compliance audit—third-party or internal? How often is this done? Yearly, as a minimum, would be advisable.

8. Noncompliance tracking—through nonconformance system.

Companies also commit to "other requirements," such as corporate standards or policies and union agreements, which may go beyond the legal requirements of the country or area your business is located in.

Other requirements can also refer to industry standards or best practices, world-class manufacturing, requirements tied to contracts/agreements, insurance, codes of ethics, and leases. These also need to be identified and managed.

Assess & Reflect #38

LEGAL AND OTHER COMPLIANCE ISSUES
Do we have any compliance issues? What are they?

❶ Quality—customer satisfaction
❷ Environment—prevention of pollution
❸ Occupational health and safety—prevention of injury and ill health
❹ Financial, etc.
❺ Other

What reporting do I review tied to compliance? Is it sufficient?

_____

_____

_____

_____

_____

_____

_____

_____

_____

_____

_____

_____

_____

_____

_____

_____

_____

_____

_____

_____

Best Practices

Best practices can be industry-committed and be benchmarks for organizations to improve to, rather than being mandated as regulatory or legislative requirements. Best practices do not necessarily produce the results that an individual organization may require, as each organization is unique and has different support structures and resources in place.

UK Government White Paper by Graham Williams

There are many articles and white papers posted on the site www.axelos .com related to best management practices. The site was created by or on behalf of the UK government (UKG) and in June 2010 came under the Cabinet Office. The products were created to help UK government organizations to develop capability and improve efficiency and deployment of best practices in their management disciplines.

One of them is entitled *Everything You Wanted to Know about Management of Risk (M_o_R) in Less Than 1,000 Words*, by Graham Williams (December 2011). He writes that effective risk management satisfies the first seven of the principles listed below. The eighth principle is the result of the risk management implementation.

1. Aligns with objectives
2. Fits the context
3. Engages stakeholders
4. Provides clear guidance
5. Informs decision making
6. Facilitates continual improvement
7. Creates a supportive culture
8. Achieves measurable value

I do support Graham Williams' white paper; however, I would suggest the addition of one more step to the process model of management of risk in Figure 4.1, and that is to add "Improve" to his "Identify, Assess, Plan, Implement" process from *Management of Risks: Guidance for Practitioners*.

As a leader you need to know the risks, and to act to improve the minimization of the risks. The Axelos site offers many interesting perspectives and encourages innovation within the management of the government.

Compliance Costs

Managers are held accountable for regulatory requirements, and fines for violations can be considerable. These are examples of some of the large organizations that have been charged in North America. Many of these organizations have been in existence for many years and still, without the watchful eyes of government, have not implemented programs to improve environment and health and safety risks.

No matter if you are a small, medium-sized, or large organization, it is key to identify the risks tied to your company and implement a plan of action for managing them, prior to being charged. In some cases these charges can put you out of business.

The watchful eyes of government officials have helped in North America; however, in many other countries, standards and regulations are not in place or are not at the same levels as in Canada or the United States.

There may be cheaper labor in other countries; however, the environmental conditions are not the same. For example, soil contamination levels and air pollution levels are high in some of these countries. Food is being grown in these areas, where cheaper labor exists, yet irrigation is being done with gray water, which would not be allowed in North America. These food items are then exported to North America. Is North America lowering its standards? We now import not only food products but also materials that are cheaper because they use materials and processes that governments in North America have banned.

A solution may be to have governments put a tax (tariff) on products being imported that do not meet the quality standards that are required in North America? If so, verification through an audit process would be a new business, bringing international standards for product manufacturing and food processing in those countries.

Barrick Sudamerica

On May 25, 2013, CBC News reported on Barrick Sudamerica Gold in Chile's Pascua-Lama being fined one of the highest environmental fines in Chile's history—$16.4 million. The Diaguita Indians live in the foothills of the Andes, just downstream of this gold mine.

The story tells of the enormous quantity of cyanide Barrick works with and the impact on the glacier-fed river, which they believe is contaminated and drying up. This river irrigates their orchards and vineyards and feeds their animals. There were complaints by the Indians of cancerous growths and aching stomachs.

This small community united to defend their rights to "not take away their water and end their culture," as quoted in the article.[2]

Cabot Corporation

The chemical industry is another sector under the watchful eye of government and the public.[3] Cabot Corporation, which is headquartered in Boston, Massachusetts, on November 19, 2013, agreed to spend over $84 million to control harmful air pollution in three facilities in Louisiana and Texas. It is the second largest carbon black manufacturer in the United States, which includes rubber additives for tires and brake pads, activated carbon for air purifiers, and chemicals used in the manufacturing of lithium-ion batteries and inkjet colorants.

The company operates in over 20 countries, with 36 manufacturing plants. It will pay a civil penalty of $975,000 as well, related to controlling harmful air pollutants that can cause serious long-term respiratory harm.

The EPA has been focusing on enforcing emissions reductions at carbon manufacturing plants in the United States and ensuring pollution control technology. The 15 carbon black manufacturing plants in the United States do not have controls of SO_2 and NOx and do not have continuous emissions monitors.

City of Shreveport

Another example of fines announced by the EPA and Department of Justice is the City of Shreveport, which agreed to do significant upgrades to reduce overflows from its sanitary sewer system.

They were required to pay a $650,000 civil penalty to resolve Clean Water Act (CWA) violations stemming from illegal discharges of raw sewage.

Shell Oil

The EPA reported on July 10, 2013, that "Shell Oil and affiliated partnerships (Shell) have agreed to resolve alleged violations of the Clean Air Act at a large refinery and chemical plant in Deer Park, Texas, by spending at least $115 million to control harmful air pollution from industrial flares and other processes, and by paying a $2.6 million civil penalty.

"Shell has agreed to spend $1 million on a state-of-the-art system to monitor benzene levels at the fence line of the refinery and chemical plant near a residential neighborhood and school and to make the data available to the public through a website."

Walmart Stores, Inc.

Walmart, the largest retail company in the world, is another organization cited on the U.S. Environmental Protection Agency (EPA) enforcement page, with civil violations of the Resource Conservation and Recovery Act (RCRA) and the Federal Insecticide, Fungicide and Rodenticide Act (FIFRA) for management of hazardous waste at Walmart stores across the country and mismanagement of damaged pesticide containers.

Prior to 2006 Walmart did not have a program in place for managing hazardous wastes at its locations, which would include identification, proper handling and storage, manifesting, emergency response requirements, and proper disposal. This civil penalty cost it $7.6 million in civil penalties to the United States.

Owens-Brockway Glass Container Inc.

The EPA and Department of Justice ordered the Ohio-based Owens-Brockway Glass Container Inc., the nation's largest glass container manufacturer, to pay a $1.45 million penalty to resolve alleged Clean Air Act violations at five of the company's manufacturing plants.

It agreed to install pollution control equipment to reduce harmful emissions of nitrogen oxide (NOx), sulfur dioxide (SO_2), and particulate matter (PM) by nearly 2,500 tons per year at its five facilities in Atlanta, Georgia; Clarion, Pennsylvania; Crenshaw, Pennsylvania; Muskogee, Oklahoma; and Waco, Texas.

Companies making modifications to their equipment, such as furnaces, get preconstruction permits, which the organization did not do. The company is spending an estimated $37.5 million on controls to reduce emissions of NOx, SO_2, and PM and installing continuous emission-monitoring equipment.

What is important related to these charges is that NOx can cause or contribute to many different types of health problems and impact ground-level ozone, acid rain, global warming, etc.

Compliance Costs—Employee Penalties

Fines are not always directed at employers; employees are fined for safety violations as well. Do you have meeting compliance requirements as one of your ongoing objectives?

There is legislation in place in some of Canada's provinces allowing government officers to issue fines from $100 to $500 to workers and employers and administrative tickets up to $10,000 for repeat offenders.

Some of the factors that determine the penalty by the officer include: the seriousness of the contravention or failure to comply, the risk of harm resulting from this, and other factors the officer considers relevant.

These fines, which will come into effect in 2014, may be a money-maker for government, but they also are a tool to promote safe work practices and an incentive to ensure the worker, as well as the company, is accountable.

However, if employees are fined, will they report injuries? Supervisors are also subject to fines—how will they be judged, working between the employer and employees? Should they be charged for a worker being exposed to workplace hazards?

We do know that employees play an important role in workplace safety; however, this type of policy does not exist in the United States. OSHA places responsibility for a safe and healthy workplace on employers, who are required to comply with occupational safety and health standards under the act.

Strategic Planning—Objectives and Programs

Continual improvement of the organization's overall performance is a permanent objective for any company.

Senior management is responsible for ensuring that objectives tied to the management of its risks are established throughout the organization and that there is a system in place to track and monitor them. These objectives need to be consistent with the company's policy statement(s) and take into consideration customer satisfaction, new projects or new/modified activities, products, services, or legal requirements. Organizations have many objectives, from improvement of operations, meeting customer requirements, and improving product realization to improving sustainability and enhancing occupational health and safety (reducing incidents and accidents).

1. Determine the tools used for managing and tracking business performance throughout the organization.
   - Six Sigma
   - Lean manufacturing
   - Quality cost analysis
   - 5S
   - Kaizen
   - Cost accounting
   - Benchmark studies
   - Business plans

- Customer satisfaction surveys
- Objectives—improvement
- Award recognition

2. Determine and prioritize plans for the upcoming year and the long term (two to three years), looking at the inputs and outputs. If plans are too far away in time, support is sometimes difficult to get from team members—the buy-in is not there.

3. Questions to ask:

   a. Are the objectives consistent with the policy?

   b. What objectives do you have in place for:

      i. Quality

      ii. Environment

      iii. Health and safety

      iv. Other

   c. Who is responsible for overseeing them? Is there an action plan in place? Are they tied to a budget requirement?

   d. Are objectives measurable? Are time lines tied to them?

   e. Is there buy-in for your objectives? Which one is done and why?

   f. Are they realistic to achieve?

   g. How are objectives and targets tracked and reviewed for completion?

4. Addressing risks—establish objectives with measurable indicators and continual improvement projects. Take into account risks and their significance, looking at the severity and frequency of impacts, together with legal requirements and opportunities to change.

5. Management of change—plan to manage change in a systematic way, reviewing the potential consequence of the changes and ensuring that knowledge needs are considered.

6. Determine key performance indicators (KPI)—these metrics or indicators will ensure tracking of progress and that improvements are managed with accountability.

7. Determine monitoring requirements for objectives and targets (O&T)—daily/weekly/monthly, depending on progress to ensure ongoing alignment with the plans.

8. Determine communication channels for informing stakeholders about progress—executive planning strategies can be communicated to employees through company meetings, intranet, and postings.

9. Management review process—one of the key areas for planning to consider is that the organization wants to improve; therefore the management system structure continues with each project in each management system cycle (quarterly, yearly, etc.), and we ensure that we identify, insure, and improve.

Good to Great

Jim Collins describes the planning stage well in his book *Good to Great*, outlining the "hedgehog concept," which is an operating model that reflects the understanding of three intersecting circles:

1. What you can be the best in the world at

2. What you are deeply passionate about

3. What best drives your economic or resource engine

Assess/Reflect/Act

In the beginning of the book, you assessed and reflected on principles. Now it is time to take action to commit your company to being innovative, to improving, and to be sustainable.

This may require improvement in your management system structure, processes, risk reduction, resources, direction for the organization, and so on.

- Who will champion them?
- Time frame—*act now*.
- Investment—what value does it bring?

Assess & Reflect #39

WHAT KEY OBJECTIVES DO I HAVE FOR IMPROVEMENT AT OUR ORGANIZATION? ARE THEY MEASUREABLE?
WHAT CHANGES AM I MAKING IN OUR WORLD?

_____

_____

_____

_____

_____

_____

_____

_____

_____

_____

_____

_____

_____

_____

_____

_____

_____

_____

_____

_____

_____

_____

_____

Notes

1. Western Digital Technologies. "Global Citizenship; Letter from the CEO." Available at: www.wdc.com/en/company/globalcitizenship /ceoletter.aspx.
2. The Canadian Press. "Canadian mine giant Barrick fined a record $16.4M in Chile," May 25, 2013. Available at: http://www.cbc .ca/m/touch/business/story/1.1308099.
3. Fines are posted on the EPA government website: http://cfpub.epa .gov/compliance/cases/.

CHAPTER 13

Step Two: Insure

Implementation of Plans

Now that you have identified your strategic plans, you need to have your "support" processes in place to carry out the organization's policy, goals, and planned objectives and targets to improve business operations.

Support is essential for the success and sustainability of your business, and needs to be managed. Applicable documentation needs to be put in place, resources and infrastructure requirements outlined, and controls implemented for documented information (IT, procedures, work instructions), communication systems, and appropriate training (knowledge, competence).

In this step, employees, contractors, and visitors are educated about the applicable risks. These may be tied to their work or to working in a safe environment, following applicable procedures or work instructions.

When incidents or accidents occur, investigations take place to ensure mediation takes place. Inspections are key to ensure ongoing conformance to requirements. Managers are to take every precaution reasonable for the protection of the workers and the company. They will determine root causes and plan to manage corrective actions related to nonconformances.

Employees also have a responsibility for the quality of their work, to prevent the occurrence of product/service nonconformity, to assist in identifying any risks tied to not only quality but also environment and health and safety, which contributes to the well-being of the organization, and to provide input about improvement.

Agent for Innovation

Innovation is crucial not only for the growth of an organization but also for the ability to sustain its viability in the competitive global marketplace. Support from everyone in the organization is needed; your culture needs to promote and live innovation as a mindset.

You as a leader must take part and have active involvement in innovation, encouraging your people to think independently and creatively to be innovative agents. When a new idea is presented by your people, how do you encourage the execution of it? How is it rewarded? What innovation has your organization done related to new products/services and value for your customer?

InnovationPoint—Leapfrogging

There are many excellent books, as well as papers on innovation. Soren Kaplan is author of the bestseller and award-winning book *Leapfrogging*. He, along with Derrick Palmer, are founders of InnovationPoint, and their work has assisted major organizations, such as Disney, PepsiCo, Frito-Lay, Kimberly-Clark, Red Bull, Colgate-Palmolive, Medtronics, Phillips, Hewlett-Packard, Merrill Lynch, and Wells Fargo.

A strategic innovative approach, InnovationPoint outlined in their white paper called *A Framework on Strategic Innovation*, "starts with the end in mind," identifies long-term opportunities, and then "bridges back to the present." Innovation is a systematic managed approach and needs to be a repeatable process.

Seven Dimensions of Strategic Innovation

As outlined in InnovationPoint's white paper, the seven dimensions of strategic innovation are:[1]

1. **A Managed Innovation Process:** Combining nontraditional and traditional approaches to business strategy
2. Strategic Alignment: Building support
3. Industry Foresight: Understanding emerging trends

4. Consumer/Customer Insight: Understanding articulated and un-articulated needs
5. Core Technologies and Competencies: Leveraging and extending corporate assets
6. Organizational Readiness: The ability to take action
7. Disciplines Implementation: Managing the path from inspiration to business impact

Support—Resources

Support is crucial for the successful management of the business and must be managed. Information plays a significant role in making quality managerial decisions; therefore managers should cultivate and encourage the proper management of support processes and carefully select the individuals who will control these areas, ensuring customer satisfaction.

Management needs to have laid the foundation with adequate policies and framework so that systematic tools and timely information can be applied for decision making and taking necessary actions at appropriate times.

Management information software systems give managers quick access to information. They provide the ability to be programmed to perform routine checks to automatically discover deficiencies, which can improve efficiency of a company's operations, saving time and resources and improving profitability. Automation of information allows multiple users to access information across the organization to verify or question the details. Accountability is also instantaneous.

Organizational Roles, Responsibilities, and Authorities

Employees at all levels of the organization are the essence of success in meeting customer requirements and business success.

One priority above all others in managing a business is to acquire as many of the best people as you can. The single biggest constraint on the sustainability or success of an organization is the ability to get and to hang on to enough of the right people. I cannot emphasize enough the importance of the grey tsunami for your organization, as many skilled managers and technical people will be leaving the workforce.

You as a leader of your organization need to address succession planning for replacement of these key business leadership individuals while your managers are still in place. This gives an opportunity for them to mentor the new replacements. Should you be an owner of a small business, you need to not only consider succession planning but also address business exit planning to design a strategy for the continuation of the business and not necessarily the sale or closure of it.

To manage effectively, it is important to provide a clear definition and understanding of roles and competencies required for the functions, accountability, responsibilities, and interrelationships in the workplace in order for your people to be dynamic. Failing to define this information can result in miscommunication and misunderstandings, which result in inefficiencies within your business. When people are unsure of what is required of them, this will cost companies time and money.

- Determine resources to implement and communicate information
- Management representative(s) appointed
- Team approach
- Organizational chart
- Job descriptions/talent management/assessment planning
- Succession planning
- Business exit planning

Assess & Reflect #40

ORGANIZATIONAL ROLES, RESPONSIBILITIES, AUTHORITIES SUCCESSION PLANNING—THE GREY TSUNAMI

How many employees will retire in next three to five years?

What succession planning is in place?

What time frame is needed to have the new replacements take over top positions?

_____

_____

_____

_____

_____

_____

_____

_____

_____

_____

_____

_____

_____

_____

_____

_____

_____

_____

_____

_____

Role of the Boss

Senior management oversees the management of company's operations, ensuring resources are available, including financials, people, resources, equipment, etc. and that cost controls are in place. One of their critical responsibilities is the analysis of data and the ongoing monitoring and review of the effectiveness and efficiency of the company's operations.

Managers and supervisors need to know and apply the organization's policy and applicable legal requirements. They need to carry out the plans to meet the objectives and targets for their areas and continually improve through analysis of data and input to the management reviews.

They need to ensure that employees in their areas understand the risks tied to their work area and any legal requirements and implications. They ensure that employees have a safe work environment, taking every precaution reasonable for the protection of the workers. They ensure employees work in a safe manner, following the organization's applicable work instructions or procedures.

Overseeing that direct employee training needs are being managed may also be their responsibility, although some organizations have human resources departments managing this area as well, covering orientation training; skills training; environment, health and safety training; and emergency preparedness.

Monitoring and measurement are important to the ongoing workings of a company, whether to incorporate requirements, customer specifications, or legal requirements. Review may be done through management review, inspections, reports, etc.

Managers and supervisors are also responsible for investigating any nonconformances tied to not following requirements and determining the root cause of the situation so that they can outline corrective and preventative actions.

Employees—Engagement and Innovation

As outlined in the principles earlier in the book, it is important for employees/contractors to work in an environment that would allow for engagement and innovation.

The direct relationship your employees have with their managers or supervisors may impact your business, as most employees leave a company due to the relationship they have with them.

An organization needs its people at all levels of the organization to be engaged and responsible for improving the effectiveness and efficiency of the company's operations, and to assist in identifying improvement opportunities and bringing forward product/service nonconformities so that they can be addressed. The hands-on people usually know what the issues are, such as problems tied to product quality, and understand the environment, health, and safety risks of their work.

The following five questions may help you have a better understanding of your employees and review your support system for engagement and innovation.

1. What are your core values? This I emphasized in the beginning of the book. Do your employees know what you have set as the core principles or values?

2. Does their work environment enable active participation to meet the guiding principles or values that you have set as leaders of the organization? What successes have you had? Why?

3. Does your organization coach employees, aligning them with your organization's objectives for continual improvement to drive your business mission? How?

4. How do you measure and improve your workforce engagement so that innovation is part of the culture?

5. Do you recognize the people working for you for their contributions and achievements to these values? How?

Recognition

Innovation is needed to help business with not only solving problems but also coming up with creative ideas to improve or create value for the organization. It is important to recognize the individual(s) at the time of the input or when a project has been completed, not just at an awards ceremony at the end of the year, which has been the case with many companies in the past.

Ongoing recognition is important to build relationships with your employees, to understand their passions, and to make them feel like valued members of the team by being creative change agents. A happy employee will help an organization be more productive, and is eager to contribute every day.

Today's companies have been more supportive of employees by providing opportunities for them to work from home, as well as working extended four-day weeks. Top performers look to work with companies that respect and can meet their needs, as well as the organization's.

In the future, with the shortage of talent, companies will need to find ways to attract and keep good employees, not only providing a quality work experience but also providing the security that they will need to work with their company.

Building Employee Relationships

To build employee relationships, it is important for you as a manager or leader to have an understanding of what matters to your employees, why, and how it can impact your productivity. Where does your organization stand related to these areas?

It is the day-after-day interactions that are key. When Towers Watson examined which behaviors influenced an employee's view of manager effectiveness, these top three emerged:

1. Manager assigns tasks suited to employee skills.
2. Manager clearly communicates goals and objectives.
3. Manager encourages new ideas and new ways of doing things.

This report shows that an effective relationship with one's direct manager can support engagement and energy.

Assess & Reflect #41

WHAT ARE MANAGERS AND SUPERVISORS DOING TO BUILD EMPLOYEE RELATIONSHIPS?

HOW AM I ENCOURAGING AND REWARDING EMPLOYEE ENGAGEMENT?

1. What are our core values? This was emphasized in the beginning of the book. Do our employees know what our core principles or values are?
2. Does their work environment enable active participation to meet our guiding principles or values that I have set for the organization? Successes?
3. Do we coach employees, aligning them with our organization's objectives for continual improvement to drive business success? How?
4. How do we measure and improve our workforce engagement so that innovation is part of our culture?
5. Do we as a company recognize and reward the people working for us for their contributions and achievements regarding these values? How?

_____

_____

_____

_____

_____

_____

_____

_____

_____

_____

_____

_____

_____

_____

_____

Assess & Reflect #42

HOW AM I ENCOURAGING EMPLOYEE INNOVATION?

_____

_____

_____

_____

_____

_____

_____

_____

_____

_____

_____

_____

_____

_____

_____

_____

_____

_____

_____

_____

_____

_____

_____

_____

_____

_____

Future Competencies in Demand

Studies such as those done by Towers Watson have shown that employee recognition improves or builds performance and keeps employees with the organization.

A study called "Global Talent 2021," conducted by Oxford Economic, with support from Towers Watson and other global employers, outlined the new competencies that would be in high demand in the future:

- Digital skills: Working virtually and using social media
- Agile thinking: Ability to deal with complexities and ambiguity, so they can assess and plan for multiple scenarios; interpersonal skills; effective physical and virtual teaming and collaboration
- Global operating ability: Including managing diverse groups of people, understanding international markets, being culturally sensitive[2]

Resources–Training–Competence–Awareness

A successful organization, it is said, is only as good as its people. Great leaders think about who is on the team, ensuring they have the right competent people to implement, maintain, and improve the management system's effectiveness, and to ensure and enhance customer satisfaction.

It is top management who ensures availability of resources and information to support their policy and objectives, measured by key performance indicators. Responsibilities need to be defined, documented, and communicated, and evidence of competence is required.

Resources need to be allocated against forecast requirements, and reviewed and supplemented if required. Determine what resources will be outsourced, and why. These resources may also include outsourcing the internal audit function, as well as the third-party audits. Should you decide to have your own internal audit team, you need to ensure that your auditors are trained on the updated new management system structure, ISO 9001:2015.

These people need awareness of how the management system structure works, and of the process risks, legal requirements, and implications of not conforming to its requirements. They need to understand the organization's policy and objectives, as well as their role in making the organization successful and realizing their own full potential, or they will leave an organization dissatisfied.

Training requirements need to be determined not only for management and personnel but also for contractors. Managers and team leaders need to ensure that employees are appropriately trained and have access to the tools and resources required to do their jobs.

There are many types of training performed by organizations, from orientation training covering the company's policies, risks, and rules associated with conducting business to on-the-job training, as well as professional development training. With management system implementation, there are training requirements for standard requirements, auditor training, and emergency preparedness training. The need for training can be the result of introducing a new technology, cross-training, new procedures or work instructions, understanding risks tied with tasks, nonconformities found in the workplace tied to the process, employee performance results, or the hiring of new or part-time employees.

Depending on the size of the organization, the management of training records and delivery can be organized by the human resources manager, or managed by the employee's supervisor or line manager. In other cases it may be the responsibility of the environment, health, and safety manager. Records and tracking of competence are becoming more important today, and keeping track of not only training that has been provided but also identification of training needs is important.

Organizations need to attract the most competent people, and these people want to work with an organization that has a meaningful purpose. In today's marketplace, companies need creativity and innovation and therefore they need to provide a safe and encouraging environment where employees can propose new ideas and contribute; this is important, rather than the old school of "don't make mistakes" and "don't take chances."

The organization provides and maintains infrastructure (buildings, workspace, process equipment, supporting services) as well as its work environment (safety rules, ergonomics) to achieve conformity of goods and services and regulatory requirements. It also ensures availability of resources and information necessary to support operation and monitoring of processes.

One of the organization's focuses is eliminating or minimizing risks to personnel and other interested parties who could be exposed to environmental impacts and or occupational health and safety hazards tied to the organization's processes. Employees can participate in understanding hazards and risks through training or one-point lessons.

A one-point lesson is a fabulous tool, and takes only about 10 to 15 minutes to develop and about the same time to present. The lesson is developed by supervisors or team leaders and consists of 80 percent visuals and 20 percent words. These are important, simple lessons to improve knowledge of what or how actions are to be achieved, showing the best examples and then, if required, showing the example of what does not work. Employees make a commitment to follow these lessons, which can be documented on their training record.

Work Environment

The management of the work environment covers many areas today, from work ethics, social interaction, and languages to environment, health, and safety concerns for the workers, such as ergonomics, stresses (heat, humidity, cold), noise and lighting levels, exposure limits, indoor air quality, and cleanliness.

This area has become a huge responsibility for management, who must ensure that hazard material warnings and safety notices are posted, and that the following are provided: secured storage areas for chemicals along with spill kits, personal protective wear, and equipment, signage for confined entry, and guarding for machinery and proper procedures for areas, such as lock-out, tag-out, and documented inspections.

Without a proper management system structure in place, these areas tend not to be monitored, measured, and inspected properly. More and more regulations are coming into play to manage environment, health, and safety compliance.

Communication

A management system requires that you define how you communicate internally and externally regarding your organization.

EDP Products Limited was featured in a report called "The Changing Dynamics of Leadership," written by the Ministry of Economic Development, Trade and Employment in Toronto, Ontario. The report says that the President of EDP, Joe DeMan, did not like the headline of a news story on his company that read, "Struggling to Stay Afloat," so he printed his own title and glued it to the framed story in his office, which closely reflects his company's attitude, "Defying the Odds." Success is definitely a choice, and Mr. DeMan took a positive step to motivate and show his people what the company stood for.

It is important to put in place the structure of the managing organization's communication, not only internally but externally to other interested parties and to the world in a positive manner. Executive peer-group organizations can provide excellent networking opportunities where like-minded individuals can meet, sharing common challenges and solutions and providing professional development and mentoring, as well as opening up opportunities.

Customer Communication

Customer communication is critical and tracking of enquiries, order handling, and amendment documentation (statements, correspondence, policies), customer feedback, and complaints is so important to understand the needs of the customer and deliver better customer experiences resulting in satisfaction.

Do you know your customer? Remember the 20 percent rule. What do they value? Resources such as Google and LinkedIn help us to understand our clients, knowing more about their business.

The traditional methods of mail are being replaced by email, cloud computing, automated notifications, online chats, and social media. Customer interactions are shifting. Bills received in the mail are now viewed, saved, and paid online or on mobile devices.

Competitive Edge—Online Communication—ICT Facts

The International Telecommunication Union (ICT), based in Geneva, Switzerland, is the official source for global ICT statistics. Its latest ICT facts and figures on www.itu.int/ict showed universal growth.

> In 2013, there were almost as many mobile-cellular subscriptions as people in the world, 6.8 billion mobile-cellular subscriptions (more than half in the Asia-Pacific region – 3.5B). Mobile-cellular penetration rates stand at 96% globally; 128% in developed countries and 89% in developing countries. There are 2.7 billion people online, almost 40% of the world's population. There are more men (41%) than women (37%) online and the gender gap is more pronounced in the developing world, where 16% fewer women than men use the internet, compared to 2% fewer in the developed world.

Customers no longer need to be tied from nine to five, as they can do business at any time of the day. There is more pressure today to improve customer experiences through technology, and companies need to evaluate their business processes and supporting technology systems to see what will give them that competitive edge. This technology comes with a substantial investment, and costs can range from a few hundred thousand dollars to a few million dollars.

Business notifications to customers can be done through automated communication, either by voice, text, or email, based on the urgency of the message. These calls can be initiated by parameters the company sets. For example, if invoices are over the 30-day mark or with a markdown on a product, an automated reminder or message can be sent. This type of communication can also be used by a manufacturing facility when it needs to get information out to many people quickly, such as canceling a shift due to weather conditions or unexpected shutdowns or emergencies.

It is imperative for companies to perform due diligence to ensure the technology will pay off in the long term, as technology changes quickly and unanticipated costs escalate with the need for professional services and new or updated software. This can be managed through change management and identification of the risks tied to this change.

The questions the managers may ask as part of any project are: What types of processes and applicable tasks need to be supported and in what communication channels? What information or data is required for these tasks and is there need to update or upgrade the technology for access? What are the risks tied to this change—how will it impact our business? What value does the organization receive (cost savings, profits)?

Digital Technology Transformation—Starbucks

Digital technology is a new way to be connected with customers, opening up new ways to do business. Starbucks is one company that jumped on this new medium by being innovative in introducing Wi-Fi to reengage with its customers and their digital rewards program.

The digital Starbuck's loyalty program with the Starbucks Card, according to Howard Schultz, CEO, is now a multibillion-dollar business in the Starbucks mobile platform: "Today we are now processing roughly 4.5 million mobile transactions a week, far greater than anyone in the world in our space, and that mobile platform is giving us a greater speed of service, higher attachment, higher ticket, and higher reload."

They also have a program for retail purchases that gives credit to their customers. "The Starbucks brand is succeeding today because of its unique emotional level of attachment and relevancy in the digital world [and] in the mobile world. The investments that we're going to make in those areas going forward are going to create a flywheel effect that is going to create more traffic into our stores because of the relevancy we have in people's lives outside of the four walls of Starbucks."

Digital technology has provided operating leverage to increase their revenue. To be competitive in today's marketplace, you need to flow with social media, as it is not a fad and it is here to stay. However, many companies have not and will be left behind their competitors.

You, as the president, general manager, and top management, need to practice strategic innovation to invest in new technologies now and have this on your executive agenda in order to create a clear direction to include in your management system development. This is a new era, and most companies lack experience in this area.

Leaders of today and the youth have a different mindset. Conservative companies hanging back will be lost. There are many benefits of digital technology—not just improving customer engagement (Facebook, Twitter, YouTube, blogs, etc.), but also streamlining operations, working with improved business models, or creating new lines of business for the company.

A report entitled "Embracing Digital Technology—A New Strategic Imperative," developed by Sloan Management Review and Capgemini Consulting Reach, researched over 1,500 executives in 106 countries and found that 78 percent of executives say that digital transformation will become critical to their organizations within the next two years.[3]

External Communication

An organization wants to demonstrate integrity and transparency with respect to reporting, ensuring quality of information and metrics, and engaging the appropriate stakeholders, whether it is reports on its financial status, environmental sustainability, or business reporting.

Does your organization review information prior to distribution and then does it encourage stakeholder feedback on these reports to allow improvement in the future? Many organizations today communicate their company's values, directions, and action items in "sustainability reports."

Communication with legal authorities related to permits, certificates of approvals, and reports from external insurance or compliance areas need to be documented, tracking actions (noncompliance/nonconformance) taken and by whom. Does your organization have a procedure to follow when government officials visit your organizations? Who is to communicate with them?

Internal Communication

Internal communication is the lifeblood of the organization, providing your people with information that they need to do their jobs effectively and efficiently. When information is shared across business divisions, it creates synergy so all can work with the same information and data and see the whole picture of what is happening at the organization.

Communication is a two-way exchange. It is not enough to just provide information or data; you must ensure that people understand it. There are four aspects to communicating its content: providing your people with clear standards, objectives, and work instructions; the tone in which it was delivered; the structure through which it was delivered; and the feedback to verify what is understood.

The exchange of ideas and opinions provides the opportunity for your people to be innovative. Communication is one of the most important aspects of managing your business, which can improve it, keeping everyone informed and allowing the company to respond appropriately, whether by problem solving or improving good relations with your people.

Does your organization promote a sense of ownership of working toward the company's goals? Are problems or issues related to process areas brought out into the open for discussion? If not, how can they be resolved?

Knowing what information needs to be provided and by whom and to whom is important. Evaluating the systems that the organization has in place also enables internal communication.

What is the information you want to convey to your visitors? Will the policy statement be sufficient? How do you inform them of the risks tied to visiting your company, such as environment, health, and safety, as well as emergency preparedness? What is the culture of the organization (its accepted ways of doing things—meetings to allow contact of personnel, dress codes, etc.)?

Internally, companies need to communicate their policy and their strategic plans so that all can be aligned to meet the goals of the organization. Leaders need to communicate to the interested parties the importance of meeting customer and statutory and regulatory requirements. Employees understand the risks tied to their work and need to provide input into management decisions tied to process changes, materials, working conditions, and environment, health, and safety issues.

Verification of Communication

To ensure that communication is relayed throughout the organization, internal auditors can ask a sampling of employees and contractors how the individual's work relates to achieving the company's policies and objectives.

- Do they have an understanding of the organization's values and directions, and what the main objectives are for the company? Have they given input into innovative changes in the company? What are they?
- Do they have an understanding of job related risks and procedures tied to their work? Were they involved with the identification of hazards, risk assessments, and determination of controls?
- When changes occur within the organization that affect them, how is communication of this change managed?
- What are the communication avenues when there is a departure from procedures or specifications (formal corrective action system)?

The most important thing in communication is hearing what isn't.
Peter Drucker (Austrian-born American Management
Consultant, Educator, Author)

Assess & Reflect #43

WHAT MESSAGES AM I COMMUNICATING TO:

- **Employees?**
- **Customers?**
- **Stakeholders?**

IN WHAT MANNER DO I COMMUNICATE THESE MESSAGES?
WHAT VALUE IS IT TO THEM?

_____

_____

_____

_____

_____

_____

_____

_____

_____

_____

_____

_____

_____

_____

_____

_____

_____

_____

_____

_____

_____

_____

Documented Information

Management systems meeting international standards for quality have in the past been very document-intensive. This discouraged many organizations from implementing the international standard. Now with the advent of electronic technology and software programs to manage business systems, the need for documented procedures is becoming irrelevant.

The new ISO 9001:2015 supports these changes in business by making reference to the term "documented information," which includes documents and records instead of documented procedures. Management standards now will be following the generic format for management systems, Annex SL, outlined earlier, which will make it easier for integrating information in a business management system manual. An organization needs to have a procedure for creating, updating and controlling its documented information.

Day-to-Day Business Management—Tell Your Story

An Integrated Management System (IMS) manual or-Business Management System (BMS) manual provides an overview of your organization's approach to business, your commitments (to quality, environment, health, and safety), identification of company's risks, referencing processes/procedures/records, responsibilities, and key systems for managing operations, and where to locate information.

This manual can be used in orientation training to introduce the company's operations to new employees or contractors, instead of duplicating time and costs in preparing new documents. It will also provide ongoing reference information for personnel. Upkeep of one centralized document (manual) helps personnel to know where to look and keep track of changes within the organization. Improved system operations will result as employees will know where to look for applicable information or procedures and records.

Not only will new employees have a road map to the company, but also it will benefit external stakeholders, such as boards of directors, government inspectors, insurance personnel, ISO auditors, etc., who will be able to understand day-to-day management of the organization.

The manual will provide a document that can provide due diligence in the case of a legal issue tied to the management of your business. Many organizations that have had compliance issues were required by judges to put in place management systems meeting international standards. Your manual will show a judge that the company has taken reasonable steps to identify and manage its risks tied to legal requirements, which provides a good start for a defense for due diligence, outlining your commitment to manage and monitor compliance issues.

Your manual will also be used by registrars/auditors who are conducting internal or third-party assessments of the organization. Does your manual tell the story of how you manage your business?

BMS or IMS Documented Information

Your BMS manual or IMS manual, whatever you wish to call it, should include the sections outlined in the following "Business Management System Manual Content Example." (Refer to Figure 13.1.)

Note: This is a manual template that would outline the core requirements for integrated management systems meeting international standards. Your company needs to adapt this template to your particular organization.

Consider the following: What is the purpose of your manual? Who will use it and why? The manual needs to be a living document, not one that just sits on the shelf or online and is never utilized.

The manual can be written by your management system coordinator or representative, or you may hire a subject matter expert on international standards for quality, environment, and health and safety or integrated management systems. His or her knowledge and advice would assist you greatly, regardless of whether you wish to register your system. This way your manual will meet the ISO criteria that have been developed by industry experts around the world and supported by more than 190 countries. The standards were developed to help companies manage their business operations in an effective and efficient manner through continual improvement.

There are many templates of manuals available online, and your management system coordinator can research these for other approaches.

The outline in this book provides the table of contents, which will address the requirements for the new generic management system for quality management, which will be released in 2015. Whichever template you utilize, ensure that all areas listed in the table of contents in the following pages are addressed.

When outlining your management system(s) in each of these categories, specify who is responsible for the overall area and the applicable documents (procedures/records) or software programs, and databases where information is kept. It is important to describe the interaction of your processes, which can be outlined in diagrams or process flow charts.

The numbering system is important in a manual, especially if you decide to register your management system. The new management system outline was described earlier, and this template follows the numbering system for the quality management system (ISO 9001-2015).

Do a draft manual, have all management review it for accuracy and clarity, and adjust as needed before it is approved and released. As changes occur, reference them in the manual, showing the revision history and status of the document and keeping it updated and current.

It is your organization, and regardless of whether you choose to go for ISO registration, you want your information to be complete and applicable to your unique operation. This way, the structure of what you have in place for managing your business will be understood around the world.

Business Management System Manual

BMS MANUAL CONTENT EXAMPLE

❶ Introduction
    a. Purpose of the manual (company developed and implemented the manual to outline its integrated MS so that the organization could provide products/services that meet customer and applicable legal requirements and be effective

(continued)

BMS Manual Content Example (continued)

and efficient enough to manage its business risks for quality, environment, and health and safety)

b. Scope (What your management system includes: all locations, one division/department, or the whole organization)

c. Exclusions (e.g., design and development—outline justification for its exclusion)

d. Outsourcing (what is outsourced?)

e. Pictures of your goods and services

f. Site diagram—locations

g. Diagram of management system processes

h. Process flow charts—outlining interaction of processes of operation

(Note: You may wish to provide the foregoing information for (d) through (g) in this section or under #4, context of the organization.)

❷ Normative references

This would outline what specific standards your management system is set up to, such as ISO 9001, ISO 14001, OHSAS 18001, etc.

❸ Terms, definitions, and abbreviations

Every company has specific key terms and abbreviations; it is helpful for those working with the company to understand what they mean.

The following are excerpts from ISO standard definitions. Adjust according to your needs.

Management system: A set of interrelated or interacting elements used to establish policy and objectives, and to achieve those objectives; a process approach to managing and controlling inputs and outputs from its processes. A management system includes organizational structure, planning activities, responsibilities, practices, procedures, processes, and resources.

Quality: Degree to which a set of inherent characteristics fulfills requirements. Quality management includes planning, control, assurance (QA), and improvement.

Environment: Surroundings in which your organization operates, including air, land, water, natural resources, flora, fauna, humans, and their interrelation. Note that surroundings in this context extend from within an organization to the global system.

Occupational health and safety: Conditions and factors that affect or could affect the health and safety of employees, or other workers (including temporary workers and contract personnel), visitors, or any other person in the workplace.

Hazard: Source, situation, or act with a potential to harm in terms of human injury or ill health or combination of two. Table 13.1 outlines common hazards.

TABLE 13.1	
Common Hazards	
Chemical	Mists/aerosols, gases, vapors, fumes, smokes, dust/fibers. Toxic, corrosive, explosive, reactive, unstable, carcinogenic, reproductive hazard, irritant, sensitizing, nerve or tissue damage.
Biological	Bacteria, viruses, fungi, molds, mites, insects, parasites, plant, animal, blood.
Mechanical	Machine parts—unguarded; moving parts; falling objects or products; moving objects—forklifts, motor vehicles.
Physical	Excess noise, extremes in temperature—heat/cold, illumination, vibration pressure, radiation, ultraviolet (UV), dust, electrostatic charges, electrical, odor.
Ergonomic	Repetitive motion injury (RMI)—poor posture; lifting—back ache/strain—heavy loads, improper manual material handling; fatigue—incorrect seating or work equipment; perceptual confusion or overload, eyestrain/headaches—poor lighting, glare/flicker on computer screen.
Fire	Fuel sources—flammable, combustible, ignition sources.
Special	Weather, earthquakes, tornado, confined spaces, air supply, unfamiliar worksites.

❹ **Context of the organization**
   a. Understanding the organization and its context (e.g., management system process diagram)
   b. Understanding needs and expectations of interested parties
        Outline the values of the company and its mission—what standards (are you registered to any, when) or what best management practices does your organization follow?
        Note: you can put the "Scope" here instead of introduction and the listing of the organization's processes.
❺ **Leadership**
   a. **Commitment**
        What commitments have you made, as the president or CEO, for your organization?

(continued)

BMS Manual Content Example (continued)

When you have an integrated management system you are making many commitments, from providing a management system structure that will meet international standards to providing customer satisfaction, prevention of pollution, prevention of injury or illness, etc.

Your commitment is outlined in your policy statement, and is communicated to your people so that they will understand and meet the organization's plans, objectives for improvement, and statutory and regulatory requirements.

By providing the resources required to manage the company and support the organization's structure, you are committing to the implementation and ongoing management of the business operations.

Your ongoing management reviews show the continual monitoring of the company's operations and the commitment you have made as the leader of the organization to ensure the effectiveness and improvement of the company's business.

Keeping abreast of line managers and employees about changing circumstances, nonconformances, corrective actions, and project status is necessary to lead on the necessary action items that come out of meetings. Having a documented agenda for these reviews and a system in place to track and manage action plans improves performance.

b. Policy statement(s)

If you have separate policy statements for quality, environment, and health and safety, I would recommend integration of these into one policy statement, which will reduce documentation and the time you are spending on these documents. Your time is valuable and needs to be focused and fine-tuned (see Figure 13.1).

   i. As president, CEO, or top management, what commitments are you making in your signed and dated policy statement?
   ii. How do you communicate this policy statement(s)? Outline the policy statement in the manual (or hyperlink to a stand-alone policy statement).
   iii. Is your policy statement current?
   iv. I have seen many companies who utilize the same policy statement for years with no updates, not even a date change to indicate that they have reviewed

the document and still support it. A policy statement dated back three years or more shows that the organization is not up to date.

v. Many organizations have their policy statements posted on their website. What does this convey to viewers or customers?

FieldTurf IMS Policy Statement

 **FieldTurf**
A Tarkett Sports Company

THE ULTIMATE
SURFACE EXPERIENCE

Integrated Management System (IMS) Policy

Fieldturf is the world leader in the manufacturing of synthetic turf systems for sports fields and residential landscaping, located in Calhoun, Georgia, USA.

Customer satisfaction is the reason we are in business. We are committed to aim for business sustainability and continual improvement through the effectiveness of our integrated quality, environment health & safety management systems (IMS), which adheres to international standards, and is a priority within our organization for its performance.

We commit to:
- Meet and satisfy our customer, who is our Corporate office, providing quality at the highest level for our products and services,
- Deliver excellence in products, services and solutions, providing the best performing, safest, most environmentally sustainable surfaces with the latest technologies and World Class Manufacturing (WCM) standards,
- Identify, assess, manage risks to our customer, employees, contractors and the environment,
- Provide a safe and healthy work environment for employees and those working under our control to prevent injury and ill health, maintaining a zero injury workplace,
- Protection of the environment and prevention of pollution,
- Compliance to applicable legislation and regulations and other requirements – such as corporate, industry and contractual,
- Establish, maintain and review company's SMART goals and our KPIs with performance indicators related to improving our IMS. Provide resources needed. Establish an audit program to verify our management system's effectiveness and ongoing continual improvement.
- Provide awareness of our IMS and Policy Statement through training and ongoing participation and communication, ensuring stakeholder's support in our commitment.
- Monitor, measure and review our management system on an ongoing basis and establish actions which may correct or prevent undesirable situations, ensuring risks are assessed, protecting the environment, health & safety of employees, quality of our products and that it remains relevant and applicable.

Harold McNeil, Sr. Vice-President of Operations   April 30th, 2013

Note: controlled signed copy on SharePoint and uncontrolled posted throughout facility.

Page 34 of 1	File name FTI-IM IMS Manual Rev 6
Ression date 04/30/13	
Control Type Electronic - Expires 24 hrs. after this date Feb.5,14	
Original Date 03/26/10 Printed copies are uncontrolled	

Source: FieldTurf.

BMS Manual Content Example (continued)

c. Organizational Roles, Responsibilities, and Authorities

6 Planning
   a. Risk management (quality, environment, health & safety) legal, emergency
   b. Reference to objectives/targets
   c. Management of change

7 Support
   a. Resource management (Put organizational chart here or under leadership or put in appendix. Outline overall responsibilities for maintaining management system requirements, from top management to management representative, committees, supervisors, general responsibilities for employees. Contractors are also key resources.)
   b. Human resources—competence
   c. Infrastructure
   d. Documented information
   e. Awareness
   f. Communication

8 Operation
   a. Operational planning and control
   b. Determining and reviewing requirements for products and services (customer communications, risks, legal and other emergencies)
   c. Design and development of products and services (this may be an exemption)
   d. Control of external provision of goods and services
   e. Production and service provision (controls, identification and traceability, external property, preservation, post-delivery, control of changes)
   f. Release of products and services
   g. Control on Nonconforming process outputs, products and services
   h. Maintenance

9 Performance evaluation
   a. Monitoring, measurement, analysis, and evaluation (customer satisfaction, quality, environment, health & safety, finance)
   b. Internal audit
   c. Management review

⑩ Improvement
   a. Nonconformity
   b. Corrective action
   c. Continual improvement
⑪ Manual revision history and change record
⑫ Documentation correspondence matrix
   Note: The matrix outlines the manual's section numbers (applicable to ISO clauses) cross-referenced to key documents/data used by the organization (e.g., procedures, standard operating procedures [SOPs], database or software programs utilized for the each area—training, nonconforming products, corrective action, inspection database).
⑬ Appendix
   a. Organizational chart (example)

Documented Procedures

ISO 9001:2008 identified required documents as being the quality policy, objectives, and a manual, and there were six required documented procedures. They consisted of Control of Documents (4.2.3), Control of Records (4.2.4), Internal Audit (8.2.2), Control of Nonconforming Product (8.3), and Corrective (8.5.2) and Preventive (8.5.3) Action.

At the time of writing, the ISO 9001:2015 quality management system committee draft refers to "documented information" to refer to both documents and records. The new standard at this time does not identify any documented procedures as being required, but refers to requirements for documented information. It does, however, outline "documented information" requirements such as the scope, policy, and objectives.

The ISO 14001 environmental standard and OHSAS 18001 occupational health and safety standards can be integrated into your quality management system following the generic numbering system, as outlined in the IMS manual content example.

Work instructions provide specific information on operational activities, assist personnel in performing their tasks, and give direction on quality, environment, and health and safety concerns tied to operations. Instructions may cover outlines of assembly, inspections, or even packaging instructions.

More and more companies today have use of computers at work stations, which provide visuals that help people understand requirements. This now supports the concept that a picture is worth a thousand words. Incorporated into this can be someone giving instructions on the video.

Documented procedures are helpful to inform employees about step-by-step tasks so there is no misunderstanding as to how things are to be done and by whom. This helps to avoid confusion and minimizes duplication, but only if the procedures are kept up to date.

Having documented procedures in place but not providing the adequate training or updates to employees will result in ineffective operations, which can result in nonconforming product/service, costing companies money.

Companies need to monitor and measure their processes to ensure that procedures are being followed. This is done through the internal audit process, as well as monitoring through inspections.

The ISO 9001 standard identifies the need for "evidence" related to monitoring and measuring devices, competence, review of goods and services prior to commitment to supply, relevant personnel being aware of changed requirements for amendments, supplier evaluations, external provider information, and monitoring, as well as information describing the characteristics of goods and services, traceability requirements, and authorization of release of goods and services. Another example is nonconforming goods and services. The standard states that documented information must be maintained on the nonconformity, subsequent actions, and concessions. Evidence is also needed for the implementation of the audit program and its results, the nature of nonconformities, and actions taken, with the results of corrective action and management reviews.

Document Control

Document control is key to any organization, and where and how it is managed can cost a company. Later we will introduce ERP, business management software.

The development of documents can be costly; however, misfiled documents can be a company's worst nightmare. Many corporations use SharePoint, which provides document and file management with intranet portals, searches, and business intelligence. The information, however, is only as good as the setup of the filing systems and categories that can be used by employees. Searches based on keywords, if not refined, can locate hundreds or sometimes thousands of documents, if setup is not done for current and archived documents and records.

SharePoint can centralize locations for storing records and documents. Check to see where in your organization documents and records are being stored, as many companies have not only SharePoint but also databases, software programs, and other drives where individual records are kept. In some cases this information may be lost if systems go down and backup information is not part of the document management system.

The intranet portal can increase employee engagement and centralize need-to-know information.

Documented procedures need to be approved, reviewed, and kept current. Records management is so important for not only business transactions but also documented proof or evidence for compliance and reduction or mitigation of risk. Proper systems for security, retrieval, and disposal are important.

When employees leave, does the organization know where to locate documents and records that have been used by them? Are special passwords required to access these documents and is there a listing of what they are? Does the organization have a records storage plan for short- and long-term housing of records and digital information?

Many external documents and records not generated by the organization have in the past been kept in file folders in an individual's desk or filing cabinets and cannot easily be found. Does the organization have a policy for paper documents to be scanned to electronic form and maintained online?

Records management today includes access of information for not only the company but also its customers and the public, which now requires controls for confidentiality, data protection, privacy, and identity theft.

Another concern is the ability to access and read electronic records over time, as sometimes software used in creating the documents has become obsolete and new systems cannot access the information.

Around the world today, more and more disasters are occurring. Has your organization prepared a disaster recovery plan to restore critical business records and systems? The Enron/Andersen scandal brought about corporate records compliance with the US Sarbanes-Oxley Act.

Assess & Reflect #44

DOCUMENTATION
ARE YOU MANAGING YOUR DATA AS A VALUABLE RESOURCE?
CAN YOUR PEOPLE FIND DOCUMENTS/RECORDS EASILY?
WHAT ARE YOUR COSTS ASSOCIATED TO DOCUMENT MANAGEMENT?
DOES YOUR ORGANIZATION USE CLOUD COMPUTING?

_____

_____

_____

_____

_____

_____

_____

_____

_____

_____

_____

_____

_____

_____

_____

_____

_____

_____

_____

_____

_____

Operation
Sarbanes-Oxley

Publicly traded companies would benefit greatly from management system structures as, today, due to corporate corruption and investor fraud,
companies are required to report on their internal controls, as well as
financial data.

The requirements for financial reporting by the Canadian Securities
Administrators and the U.S. Securities Commission (SEC) for Sarbanes-
Oxley[4] for review of internal controls can be supported by ISO 9001
implementation and audits.

The management system structure can provide objective evidence,
from identification of risks, strategic planning, operational controls, and
procedures and practices for managing customer orders to the purchasing
of materials, processing of orders, production controls, and monitoring. This
may be a cost-effective way to meet the financial reporting requirements.

Due Diligence

A management system structure outlines the controlled environment
that is crucial for the credibility of financial information. Documentation is important to provide the evidence and assessment of effective
internal controls. As a CEO and CFO, a management system meeting international standards provides the operational control and documented information to demonstrate the activities undertaken for these
controls if tied to related financial activities.

This would require a team effort to include input from accounting
and from those involved with your finances to look at the details related
to invoicing and accounts receivable, as well as customer terms, credit
limits, inventory transactions, etc.

In addition, an international management system structure provides
support for due diligence related to civil liability. Earlier in the book, I
outlined a concern related to the grey tsunami—employees leaving due
to retirement—and whether their know-how is captured in documented
information so that operational controls will not be lost.

Operational Clauses

The seven areas that will need to be addressed under operations are the following, which are outlined in the draft of ISO 9001:2015:

1. Operational planning and control
2. Determination of requirements for products and services
3. Design and development of products and services
4. Control of externally provided products and services
5. Production and service provision
6. Release of products and services
7. Control of nonconforming process outputs, products, and services

Quality Control Plan

The operational process area for planning requires the organization to address the risks it has identified and put in place controls to manage and meet the specific management system requirements you have integrated (conformity of goods and services—Quality-ISO 9001, prevention of pollution—Environment-ISO 14001, prevention of injury—Occupational Health & Safety-OHSAS 18001, etc.). A "risk plan" can be utilized for this purpose, outlining all your process areas and the risks associated with each. Many organizations have utilized quality control plans to monitor and control suitable parameters and product characteristics to ensure products meet specified requirements.

Documented information needs to be maintained and should describe the characteristics of the goods and services, the activities to be performed, and results to be achieved. These records are maintained for objective evidence during inspections and tests, and analysis needs to be done to identify nonconformances.

The quality control plans outlined the process areas and identification of control areas: what had to be made and the quantity, how it was made, equipment, measurement and monitoring tools; what to inspect, etc. The control plan, however, did not include what the risks were associated with the tasks. Many organizations will need to spend time to identify the risks for their process areas, making the quality control plan a good tool when modified to include the risks as well.

The identification of individuals responsible for executing control for the providers of the tasks, whether they are for your employees, suppliers, or contractors, would be on your plan.

Management System Control Plan

The automotive industry uses Failure Mode and Effects Analysis (FMEA), which is a tool used to improve quality, productivity, and safety. The tool is utilized to review processes, the applicable machine or device tied to them, and the specific critical characteristics of processes. This template could be enhanced to be used as a "management system control plan."

Each line item outlines monitoring and measurement requirements. This template can be expanded upon to list the risks tied to the process for quality, environment, and health and safety and become an integrated management system control plan. By integrating, you can look at each process, understanding its risks and the legal requirements tied to it for quality, environment, and health and safety.

Many environmental legal requirements are tied to monitoring: recording and submitting reports on emissions, hazardous waste disposal volumes, spill response, and process operational requirements (e.g., temperature monitoring). The applicable work instructions and procedures necessary for the task are outlined on the control plan. These need to be carried out by trained personnel. Consistency of activities following the applicable work instructions will produce consistent outputs and results.

A management system control plan is a living document, and therefore, when changes are made to your operations, whether in design or production, it needs to be updated, showing changes, whether in specifications, resources, or the monitoring and measurement required. As personnel titles change, this needs to be updated in your plan.

Figure 12.2 is a high-level process flow diagram showing the linkages and flow of activities, from receipt of materials to inventory or process areas, production processes, assembly (if required), packaging,

FIGURE 13.2

Integrated Management System Control Plan

Process Name	P or WI	Control Method Quality Env H&S	Specs	Characteristic						Process Control Method				
				Depart. Authority	Risk	Control Item*	Inspection Method	Frequency		Control Item*	Control Value	Person Responsible	Sampling and Measure	Inspection Method

Note: Risk can be in quality, environment, or health and safety.

storage, and delivery. Include your support activities as well, such as procurement, training, etc. You can follow this process flow diagram and put the details into the control plan Figure 13.2.

Goods and Service Risk Questions

As a leader of the organization you want to ask the following questions in your goods and services provision.

Planning

a. Has operational planning included determination and review of requirements (market needs and customer requirements)?

b. Do we identify our risks as new goods and services are being planned?

c. What tools are used in this regard (e.g., quality control plans, failure mode and effects analysis, feasibility projects, capital projects)?

d. What objectives have been set in goods and services?

e. Do our performance indicators focus on reducing variations and improving our production and service provision and its related resources?

  i. Product
  - Reduction in defects—nonconforming product
  - Scrap rates
  - On-time delivery

  ii. Process
  - Reduction in setup time—run rates
  - Production scheduling
  - Operator nonconformances

Change Management

Do we review the risks tied to changes made in goods and services? When we have new software system installs, do we anticipate what impacts will or are likely to occur and what are the risks? Does our change management process address changes to specifications, process/equipment, raw material, packaging, or nonconformance (corrective action cross-references)?

Do we review the risks tied to changes of personnel or contractors?

Purchasing/Procurement

The planning process for business realization ensures that customer requirements will be met, and today most organizations manage this with automated controls. Some organizations refer to their process for purchasing under "Supply Chain Management (SCM)" or "Logistics."

The new international management system model has new terminology. It refers to "control of externally provided products and services" rather than "purchasing." Suppliers are expected to provide defect-free products/services that conform to requirements.

a. What controls need to be in place in this area? What is the potential impact of the externally provided processes, products, and services on the company's ability to meet customer and legal requirements?

Lowest end-user prices, management of resources, forecasts, shipments, and inventory should also be considered.

b. Are we dealing with approved and/or qualified suppliers? Do we maintain an approved supplier list? Are there established criteria for selection, evaluation, and re-evaluation on the basis of their ability to meet requirements for product and service quality, quantity, cost, and delivery within schedule? Who maintains performance history? Are risks reviewed tied to these suppliers? Do they meet relevant statutory and regulatory requirements? Did vendor purchases meet the limits set?

c. What needs to be outsourced?

d. How do we ensure adequate control and review of provision of products and service information according to the following items? What is the evidence that it is working correctly and meeting requirements?

- Risks—impact on quality of the final product/service provided to customer
- Electronic controls
- Documentation—quotes, purchasing documents clearly describe product and/or service, and approved. Evaluation of cost of purchased product, attachments—specifications/drawings, warranty
- Terms, logistics—delivery times, specifications
- Approvals, signatures
- Records demonstrating supplier's capability, tracking of orders, IT logon
- Acknowledgment activity
- Revised or amended purchase orders
- Nonconformance-noncompliance—corrective action process
- Product returns (nonconforming product)
- Receipt of materials, product release—verification
- Quarantine area, credits
- Supplier performance evaluations

There are specific risks that accompany global supplier relationships, from distance, transportation, and time zones to cultural differences and the reliability of their infrastructure.

Ensuring your suppliers have a management system structure meeting ISO standards would assist in supporting management of documented information.

E-Commerce Innovation Leaders

Technology and the use of the Internet have facilitated the outsourcing and globalization of the supply chain, as well as information management. Ensuring controls are in place for the reliability of e-commerce is crucial today for traceability, transparency, accessibility, responsiveness, privacy, security, etc., as we rely on software to manage our documented product information.

The international standard that addresses this area is ISO 10008:2013, "Quality Management—Customer Satisfaction—Guidelines for business to consumer electronic commerce transactions." This is referred to as B2C ECT, which is the process of buying and selling products using the Internet.

The consumer can buy at any time of the day, so there are no time restraints for shopping with merchants around the world and doing price comparisons. Payment is usually at the time of purchase, and the ability of the software today allows conversion into the consumer's local currency.

Consumers, when dealing with other countries, are uncertain about who to turn to when they experience a problem. Consumer protection has many rules, depending on the country, and is still being improved.

a. E-Commerce Innovation—Dell Computer Corp.

With innovation in global e-commerce come challenges. Many retailers now look to include e-commerce, where they can also obtain information about the buying habits of customers, such as trends in demands for product features.

One of the innovators for Internet retailers is Dell Computer Corp. Dell uses online marketing, selling computer-related products to individuals, small, medium-sized, and large businesses and government, and education and health-care organizations, and then uses software—ERP (enterprise resource planning)—for the assembly operations. This allows real-time tracking of the types of products consumers desire, assisting in planning production schedules and deliveries, and improving productivity and competitiveness.

b. Innovation—FedEx

We also have business-to-business (B2B) commerce, which includes transactions between companies. FedEx's B2B provides tracking systems that allow businesses to identify the status of their deliverables at any time. This innovation has been followed by many others. B2B can include not only products but also services and information between businesses.

Procurement Manager—Supply Chain Innovator

Is the responsibility of the person in charge of the provision of products and services one of "cost savings" or a "supply chain innovation"?

Do the people responsible for procurement have the data to explore new approaches to savings? Do they possess a working knowledge of currency, discount rates, and global economic indicators? Will they be able to develop credible financial business cases and look at what-if decision making and shareholder value? Can they provide input and deliver value to senior management in providing solutions to business problems, process improvements, performance issues, risks tied to the supply chain, and new technology solutions, as well as accurate spending intelligence?

A client I was working with had a centralized procurement system in place, and the person responsible for the area was proactive in setting an objective and target to improve procurement by reducing costs tied to their largest purchases by sourcing new areas for raw materials utilized in their project installs. By obtaining new suppliers closer to their projects they were able to save over $500,000 in one year just on freight charges.

The procurement manager now and in the near future will have many challenges in the global environment, especially in optimizing supplier relationships and providing market intelligence. This person will be required to provide more in terms of reduction in costs, compliance with industry regulations, quality performance, sustainability, and shareholder returns.

Procurement is crucial for an organization and will be a challenge in the future. Having the right talent will be important. KPMG interviewed 25 senior procurement officers and worked with the Supply Chain Resource Cooperative in North Carolina State University's Poole College of Management to identify several new roles for procurement. Their report *FUTUREBUY: Delivering Procurement Value in a Complex World* is a very interesting read. Go to www.kpmg.com/us/procurement for more information.

Production and Service Provision

Both the production and provision of services requires meeting customer specifications through an understanding of the customer's requirements. For the shareholder it is producing products at a competitive price, meeting budgetary requirements. Organizations want to be world-class suppliers.

To control production of products and services, the organization will have identified all processes, their sequences, and equipment used to produce the product or service to ensure that all risks have been identified tied to quality, environment, and health and safety. This identification is usually completed through process control flow diagrams and control plans.

a. Outsourcing

The organization needs to identify the provision of external goods and services that it outsources and then will require a risk-based approach tied to these external resources.

Many companies outsource functions in order to have specialized service providers who can provide world-class capabilities for the organization. It could be due to insufficient internal resources or time-consuming activities. These providers become valuable business partners in the management of their business and can provide support to senior executives.

It is important to understand the risks tied to outsourcing, as well as the benefits. Consider confidentiality when dealing with external services and ensure your data or know-how is protected. If you are outsourcing a key process for manufacturing your product and the company cannot deliver on time or provides nonconforming materials, this impacts not only you but also your customer and maybe your bottom line.

Ensuring that your provider has a management system in place meeting international standards enables you to know that they have systems in place to manage nonconforming products and corrective actions. You will know that they take pride and ownership in a quality product or service provision.

b. Post Delivery Activities

Your organization's post-delivery activities, under ISO, include: risks associated with the products and services, requirements, warranty provisions, contractual obligations, such as maintenance, outsourcing processes, such as packaging, or services, such as delivery, recycling, or disposal. These activities are important for customer satisfaction.

c. Production Planning

Production will include the scheduling requirements taking into consideration production capacity and capability, customer delivery requirements, material and personnel availability, storage, etc.

The use of appropriate tools, such as material requirements planning (MRP) and enterprise resource planning (ERP), will assist in controlling production of goods and provision of services.

The revised ISO 9001:2015 international standard requires the need for "documented information" that describes the characteristics of the products and services and the activities to be performed and results achieved.

Documented information from everyone is essential, from the CEO and CFO to administration clerks and production, to get information on the key performance indicators (KPIs) and reports for their roles.

Documented information is necessary under operations, as outlined by the revised quality management system meeting international standards, to have the confidence that the processes have been carried out as planned:

- Evidence of the review of requirements of products and services prior to commitment to supply
- When amendments are made, evidence of relevant personnel are made aware of the changed requirements; results of evaluations of external providers (suppliers)

- Documented information to be provided to external providers
- Evidence of application of development processes, the outputs, and their suitability
- Information that describes the characteristics of products and services and describes the activities performed and results achieved
- Traceability requirements
- Results of review of changes, personnel authorizing change, and any necessary action
- Person authorizing release of products and services for delivery to customer and nature of nonconformities and any subsequent actions including concessions obtained

d. Capturing Real-Time Information

i. Enterprise Resource Planning (ERP)—Business Management Software

The key to managing today's dynamic business operations is to have systems in place to capture real-time critical information to make quick analytical decisions to gain efficiencies so that all necessary personnel are connected to the process.

Top management needs to spend monies wisely with accurate access to documented information, eliminating spreadsheet-based reporting. They need to manage business processes, from product planning and development to manufacturing, inventory, shipping, marketing, and sales to improve operations and productivity.

ERP integrates and consolidates core business processes using a database management system to track business resources, from the financial performance to streamlining materials and production capacity, the status of business transactions of sales orders, purchasing, and payroll.

Real-time data is available across all departments (supply chain, manufacturing, sales). ERP systems are based on best management practices and are usually used as is; however, vendors do offer configuration options for system customization, but these can be costly.

ii. Manufacturing ERP Index

There are many systems on the market. Choosing an operating system can be a complicated task. One of the sites on the Internet, ERP Software Systems Index for Manufacturing, outlines the top systems. It has an advisory council, which contributes to the selection and review process.

Comparisons are sorted by manufacturing modes, such as discrete, process, mixed mode, engineering to order (ETO), made to order (MTO), job shop/shop floor, light assembly, industrial and wholesale distribution, and professional services.

You can compare according to the industry as well, in such areas as aerospace and defense, agriculture, apparel, automotive, chemical, computers/electronics, consumer packaged goods, distribution, energy, food and beverage, health care/medical devices, high-tech, lumber, mining, transportation, pharmaceutical, plastics and rubber, petroleum/coal, ship building, other, and professional services.

An excellent resource is www.top10erp.org. Many of the names are well known in the industry, such as Batchmaster, Microsoft Dynamics, Infor, Sage, SAP, and Syspro. The service outlines the price range, financial options, user range, etc.

iii. Business Edge in Analytics

These IT methods combine dynamic operational analytics, to help the top management have a business edge in: planning, budgeting, providing tools for query, reporting, visualization— dashboards to improve bottom lines through supply chain management (order tracking), sales forecasting, improving inventory efficiencies, data analysis tied to production, document management, customer service, and ultimately to revenue tracking and profits. They also ensure people are connected to the processes with real-time information so they can deal with in-house changes and changing customer demands.

ERP has supported business growth for some companies up to 300 percent and integrated systems to improve order times for some clients, from 8 to 20 minutes down to 30 seconds. Additional savings were found in the area of IT development and customization utilizing an ERP system.

iv. ERP Successes

To review company stories tied to ERP, go to www.netsuite .com. Magellan GPS is quoted on its website as saying, "We have tripled our productivity, enhanced our risk management and reduced our overall Ecommerce IT expenditures by more than 20 percent."

e. Automated Control Risks

Automated control systems are evolving so that they are more integrated and scalable and can incorporate new technologies. There is networking of devices to communicate and track performance, managing process and safety controls.

Automation for industrial control systems (ICS) used in industrial manufacturing processes for Supervisory Control and Data Acquisition (SCADA) may include: Distributed Control Systems (DCSs)—controlling electric power generation, oil and gas refineries, water and wastewater, chemical, food and automotive production, or Programmable Logic Controllers (PLC), a digital computer used for automation of electromechanical processes, such as machinery on assembly lines or lighting.

It is key to identify risks tied to automation as well, such as process control security, as destruction of the systems could impact areas of society removed from the original area when tied to electric power, oil/gas, and water/wastewater and impact the health and safety of the public. These critical infrastructures are managed remotely, such as the process and distribution of water, management of electricity, operation of chemical plants, or the flow of gas and oil through pipelines, or transportation systems, like railway signaling that could malfunction.

If the automation is a software program, then access to the software would need to be controlled, as would viruses and other software threats on the host machine, with systems such as cryptographic security so an attacker does not get control of the network. There may be security needs for cyber, personnel, or physical security.

f. ISO 20000—Information Technology Service

The Information Technology Service Management international standard, ISO 20000, would help ensure controls and a framework were in place to manage security issues and to change an IT-driven culture into a business-driven culture with cost-effective services. The standard promotes the adoption of an integrated process approach, identifying the numerous linked activities and providing ongoing control, greater efficiency, and opportunities for improvement.

g. Resources—Automation

Leaders in automation include ABB and Rockwell Automation, as well as publications *Automation Today Asia Pacific*, *The Journal*, and *Automation World*.[5]

The following resources are tied to automation—organizations, webinars, publications, and trade shows:

- ISA—International Society of Automation—is a nonprofit organization setting standards for automation worldwide and certifying industry professionals, providing education and training.[6]
- The Control System Integrators Association (CSIA) is a nonprofit organization working to advance business practices of control system integration since 1994.
- The Centre for the Protection of National Infrastructure is also a good resource.[7]
- Trade shows to attend include the ABB Automation & Power World Automation Fair, where thousands of people attend.

Many government bodies are supporting innovation and productivity to help increase productivity through project initiatives. Check with your local/federal/state/provincial government to see what incentives are available.

For example, in Ontario, Canada, there is a voucher for innovation and productivity, as well as a voucher for industry.

The Inland Revenue Authority of Singapore has a list of IT and automation equipment that would qualify for enhanced deduction/allowances under its Income Tax (PIC Automation Equipment) Rules 2012, which was effective in 2011 and expanded in 2013 to qualify for 100 percent, accelerated write-offs for capital allowances.

Innovation

Green Awareness—Eco-design

Today the customer is concerned about green awareness (e.g., global warming, pollution) related to the products and services they purchase tied to their "environmental footprint" or "ecological footprint." In the area of development of goods and services, eco-design can be used to consider environmental impacts during its whole lifecycle stages (e.g., procurement, manufacturing, use, disposal), searching for new environmentally friendly solutions.

By assessing design and development, many companies improved operational costs tied to reductions of consumption of energy, materials, waste, etc.

Working together as a team, with inputs from procurement, design, production, and marketing, promotes the ability to assess environmental impacts and improve the eco-design at all life-cycle stages of the product. Product design criteria would need to be identified at each stage (e.g., resource reduction, use of recycled materials, waste recovery, reuse, longevity, etc.).

FieldTurf—Reuse of Tires—Artificial Turf

FieldTurf, a division of Tarkett Sports, has captured eco-design in the manufacturing of artificial turf. Recycled tires are used in the base for the field, and the company has addressed use of local raw materials tied to the installation, thereby reducing costs of shipping, fuel consumption, and CO_2 emissions generated from transportation. The manufacturing site based in Calhoun, Georgia, has an integrated management system, including quality, environment, and health and safety.

LEED—Green Building

It is interesting to note that the building of green architecture (building products) for commercial buildings has a Leadership in Energy and Environmental Design (LEED) rating system. This is recognized as an international mark of excellence for green buildings globally, which has redefined the green construction of buildings and communities in which people live and work.

Many countries have green building councils, which utilize the LEED rating system, as it recognizes the sustainability tied to building design, construction, and operation. Since companies have been following the LEED program, there have been astronomical savings in energy, recycling, water, etc.

The U.S. Green Building Council (USGBC) invests over $30 million a year in LEED to maintain, operate, and improve delivery to its customers (185,000+ industry professionals). It is working to help not only in saving customers money but also in conserving energy, reducing water consumption, improving indoor air quality, driving innovation, and building better material choices by as much as 40 percent.[8]

The UK design and assessment for sustainable building is "BREEAM," which was launched in the UK by BRE and has more than 110,000 certified buildings. This is an accepted standard in the UK and has been included in local plans. BREEAM builds on legislation and standards to award credits. It provides credits for complying with standard commissioning codes and meeting targets, such as Waste Management Plans (regulatory requirement in the UK). Its initiatives also include a framework that encourages project teams to stay engaged after the handover of the building to ensure that the building is running effectively.

The growing concern about "green" is seen in developing countries as well. The Asian Development Bank promotes and supports green growth in developing countries.

In 2007 China launched two national green building standards: the Green Building Design Label (GBDL) to certify the design of buildings and the Green Building Label (GBL) to certify operational efficiency.

India began green buildings prior to this, in 2004. India's developers can choose from the country's national green building system, Green Rating for Integrated Habitat Assessment (GRIHA), or LEED India.

There are many stakeholder pressures facing companies today, from environmental issues, pollution, climate change, and water quality and consumption to regulatory requirements and costs tied to operations for materials, waste, etc.

The process area within a company that deals with design and development or eco-design needs to consider not only shareholder and customer requirements but also government policies, taxes, funding incentives, competitive products/services, bank lending and liabilities, insurance risks, and concerns from the public, employees, and pressure groups as a whole in the life cycle of products and services.

By paying attention to eco-design, bottom-line benefits can occur in cost savings to material and energy use, waste reduction, and process efficiency, as well as meeting customer requirements and generating a competitive advantage for your organization. There are other marketing considerations tied to labeling energy schemes and recycling initiatives, which can provide added value to the customer and promote a competitive feature for the product/service.

Technology

NetSuite—Cloud Computing

NetSuite is a public software company founded in 1998 by Evan Goldberg and Larry Ellison. Zach Nelson has been President and CEO of NetSuite since 2002, and in 2007 the company became the leading provider of cloud computing business management software suites in the world. In 2013 he was included in the 50 Most Powerful People in Enterprise Tech list and was *Fortune*'s Businessperson of the Year in 2012. This is definitely a company with vision and an understanding of driving business sustainability and success through technology for customers, as it has over 10,000 organizations of every size in a broad range of industries.

Transparency, accessibility, and the integration of systems are crucial today to conduct business processes effectively and efficiently. Many corporations deal internationally, and cloud computing enables executives to check in on financial performance wherever they are. This type of system is excellent not only for large multinationals but also for small to medium-sized organizations that need the flexibility of accessing information.

As mentioned earlier in this chapter, working in a global marketplace requires not only the basics for accounting but also support for currency management and compliance with local regulations, taxation, and business practices. With added complexities human error definitely would increase.

The other consideration when working globally is the management of the life cycle of fixed assets, from acquisition/accounting processes to depreciation and disposition.

Assess & Reflect #45

OPERATION INNOVATION

What has our organization automated to improve operations?

How have we adopted green initiatives into our operations?

Is cloud computing a good vehicle for our company?

_____

_____

_____

_____

_____

_____

_____

_____

_____

_____

_____

_____

_____

_____

_____

_____

_____

_____

_____

_____

_____

_____

Emergency Preparedness and Response

Being prepared to take actions before, during, and after an emergency event is crucial for the safety and security of all. By identifying the risks in your process areas you have a very good understanding of what potential hazards and impacts could occur—not only the emergencies that could occur within the organization, but also how to identify and understand emergencies tied to activities with other industries adjacent to your business, such as transportation emergencies that may occur due to rail delivery adjacent to your facility.

Our business environment is also impacted by today's world, including hazards like ice storms, tornadoes, floods, hurricanes, earthquakes, accidents, acts of violence, and acts of terrorism.

The onset of health issues tied to infectious disease, such as the H1N1 flu virus (swine flu), SARS, and tuberculosis, along with technology-based hazards due to failure or malfunction of equipment, software, and systems, can also disrupt business operations.

Emergency Planning

Being prepared and planning ahead for worst-case scenarios is important. The following 11 tasks can assist you as a manager in putting together your emergency preparedness and response program to protect your employees and your business.

1. Use a team approach to identify potential emergency situations—assess risks (routine and nonroutine, such as shut-downs).
2. Identify and comply with legal requirements.
3. Identify prevention methods to reduce risks.
4. Develop an emergency preparedness plan outline—what should it include?
   - Risks
   - Resources
   - Communications—contact lists—phone numbers, alarm systems
   - Post emergency escape procedures and diagrams, such as maps outlining evacuation routes, site entrances/exits, location of

emergency equipment, fire extinguishers, spill kits, eye wash stations, chemical storage areas, and outside assembly location.

- Elaboratation on shut-down of critical plan operations—who and what.
- List notification systems—contacts.
- Specify rescue and medical duties.
- Specify offsite storage of records/documents—IT.

5. Test your emergency plan.

6. Specify training (how often and for whom). Don't forget visitors, security, and contractors.

7. Specify special equipment/supplies you need for emergencies.

8. Decide on a reporting method and clear chain of command. Consider running your accident/incidents/emergencies through your nonconformance system and categorizing the type of nonconformance for analysis. This way you have one system in place to manage nonconformities.

9. Communicate/train employees, visitors, contractors, and stakeholders.

10. Review the emergency preparedness system after: incident/accident/emergency, insurance reviews for changes and improvements.

11. What can you improve on tied to emergency preparedness?

Remember that any business disruption can have a huge impact on revenue, customers, employees, supplies, and services. When the tsunami hit Japan it was a major disaster for people living there and had a ripple effect around the world on businesses for parts and materials.

When reviewing your emergency plans, it is important to review the structure of your building to see if it will withstand natural disasters. Review changes that have occurred in building codes to support stronger construction, your maintenance practices, degradation of building materials (roofs—material types, pitch, weathering conditions, etc.).

When addressing workplace emergencies, consider your notification systems. I was in an automotive environment when there was an emergency tied to a forklift that had pulled a gas line down. The sounding of the alarm did very little for employees being notified to evacuate because of the loud noise from the stamping machines. In this case the use of lighting, as well as alarms, needs to be in place.

A workplace emergency is more than just natural disasters. It can be fires, utility failure, toxic gas releases, chemical spills, radiological accidents, explosions, or even workplace violence resulting in bodily harm and trauma. There may be an emergency tied to the railroad beside you, or your neighboring industry may be having an emergency. Working with your people to brainstorm the worst-case scenarios will assist in being prepared. Sharing your plan with adjoining businesses will help you all to be prepared and knowledgeable as to the conditions in your operation, how they could impact everyone, and what the action plan is for appropriate response.

A good, effectively managed worker health and safety program with input from employees is a big factor in reducing work-related injuries. Having ongoing inspections and third-party audits and reviews of your facility by insurance and fire departments also improves your everyday operations and preparation for emergencies.

Disaster Planning Innovation

Disaster planning is a collaborative process, and business, government, and individuals need to work together to recover from catastrophic events. This helps businesses survive and thrive and helps people live and work.

The Insurance Institute for Business and Home Safety indicates that one in four businesses never reopen following a major disaster. As more than 50 percent of the working population is employed by a small business, it is a huge impact on the economy should they not have a recovery program in place.

The "Disaster Safety Review" for 2013 is outlined in the Open for Business-EX (OFB-EZ) online program,[9] which has a free toolkit that small businesses can follow for disaster planning and recovery processes that larger companies use. This allows them to develop and store their continuity plans in a secure, third-party location, which is password-protected and accessible at any time from any location.

Technology Makes a Difference

Technology does help in an emergency. In November 2013 in the Midwestern United States, tornadoes passed over and destroyed buildings; a Methodist minister in Illinois told the story of his congregation receiving alerts on their cell phones during a church service. This alert saved the lives of over 400 worshipers, enabling them to get to a storm shelter area, while the tornado passed over, destroying buildings only yards away.[10]

The U.S. Department of Homeland Security's Science and Technology Directorate (DHS S&T) partnered with the U.S. Army to develop the Enhanced Dynamic Geo-Social Environment (EDGE) system, which allows responders to engage in simulated environments by using a video game for virtual disaster mitigation.[11] This gaming technology helps first responders, such as police and firemen, work together in a controlled environment in a virtual world.

Innovation and technology can speed up the training needed to deal with disastrous situations. Technology can truly empower every person and organization to make a difference.

San Diego County—Innovator

Where are your people when an emergency occurs?

San Diego County was an innovator and a leader, coming up with a mobile app to prepare San Diego citizens for emergencies. This area is known for its wild fires; however, it could also be hit with earthquakes, flooding, tsunamis, pandemics, and terrorist attacks. The ability to reach people with landlines or at a computer is not practical in an emergency situation; today almost everyone has a mobile device.

The county worked with a leading technology company to develop a cloud-based solution to meet virtually any load demand from wired or wireless browsers. San Diego County worked with AT&T to develop the app "SD Emergency," which keeps the public informed. The app has the ability to "push" up-to-date information about the emergency situation to app users in real time.[12]

Assess & Reflect #46

EMERGENCY—NOT BEING PREPARED

What emergency was our organization not prepared for?

What impact did it have?

What changes have been implemented?

_____

_____

_____

_____

_____

_____

_____

_____

_____

_____

_____

_____

_____

_____

_____

_____

_____

_____

_____

_____

_____

_____

_____

_____

Notes

1. For further details refer to www.innovation-point.com.

2. Global Workforce Study, "Engagement at Risk: Driving Strong Performance in a Volatile Global Environment," Towers Watson, 2012.

3. For details from the report go to www.capgemini-consulting.com /SMR.

4. For further information go to www.sec.gov.

5. Automation World. Available at www.automationworld.com.

6. The International Society of Automation. Available at www.isa.org.

7. Centre for the Protection of National Infrastructure. "Supervisory control and data acquisition (SCADA)." Available at www.cpni.gov .uk/advice/cyber/scada.

8. Those wishing to show their leadership in the green building movement may participate and register their project online: www.usgbc .org/leed/certification.

9. Insurance Institute for Business & Home Safety. Available at www .DisasterSafety.org/ofb-ez.

10. Emergency Management. Available at www.emergencymgmt.com /emergency-blogs.

11. Refer to www.emergencymgmt.com/training/Video-Game-First -Responder-Training-Edge.html.

12. For more information see the case study at http://images.erepublic .com/documents/san_diego.pdf.

CHAPTER 14

Step Three: Improve

Your organization's success is dependent on "Improve."

W. Edward Deming was quoted as saying, "If you don't know how to ask the right question, you discover nothing." Throughout the book, we have encouraged you as a leader to ask the right questions so you can analyze with the right information or data. Through analysis, you turn this information into insights for actions to take place for improvement, and then you bring value to your leadership for sustainability to business success.

The process of analysis is in Step Three, "Improve." We have reviewed the planning of the management of business operations in Step One, "Identify," and the steps required in implementing a management system structure in Step Two, "Insure." In the third step, you as a manager will look at opportunities for improvement and the systems in place that will help to direct your choices.

Senior management meets on an ongoing basis to cover key operations with a review of measureable objectives and targets, monitoring operational controls and variances and understanding nonconforming goods and services and overall improvement for the management system. Many tools have been outlined in Step One, Identify, for setting objectives to improve operations, such as Six Sigma, lean manufacturing, best management practices, reengineering, etc. Each tool can benefit your organization in serving your customer and improving the way you manage your business.

Performance Evaluation

Performance evaluations can be an effective way for managers to do the following:

1. Monitor and measure the efficiency and effectiveness of the management system structure and how it is being implemented and maintained on an ongoing basis for business sustainability.

   Establish actions to correct or prevent undesirable situations, ensuring risks are assessed in each process area. Protect the quality of product/service, the environment in which you work and the health and safety of those that work with you by monitoring requirements and being innovative with improvements to system operations, products, and services.

2. Receive feedback on the design of a project—that it has measurable objectives with indicators, provisions for collecting data and managing the project records for feedback to management for review, and realistic time frames and resources for implementation. Are projects tied to financials?

3. Receive feedback on tracking and status of projects or set objectives and targets for achieving their goals and expenditures, including process or milestone reports: date for delivery of product/ service (e.g., quarterly completion or final reporting) with output indicators—for example, time taken to process order, based on cost or operational ratios.

4. Provide guidelines or directions for planning new objectives and targets (projects) to ensure measurement tied to customer satisfaction and meeting management system commitments.

5. Identify potential risks, problems, or opportunities at an early stage and propose action items or solutions ensuring that we comply with regulatory, customer, and corporate requirements.

6. Stakeholder input—participation by stakeholders brings greater ownership for the project, encouraging and driving the business's mission. Stakeholder support early on in the process will reinforce the changes. Any problems requiring clarification and actions can take place sooner rather than later.

7. Review and understand variation in the output of each process area. Determine the factors within the process that influence the average performance.

8. Internal audits provide monitoring and verification of all management system processes. They provide inputs to management for review and suggest opportunities for improvement.

9. Compliance audits verify that we are meeting regulatory requirements and recommend improvements.

10. Management reviews inputs and outputs on a regular basis, receiving ongoing monitoring of business operations.

Monitor, Measure, Analyze, and Evaluate

Monitoring in a management system according to international standards is a commitment to focus on day-to-day management inputs and outputs and the impact of activities.

The organization needs to monitor whether process/product/legal requirements are being met in accordance to performance measurement and a predefined timetable being adhered to, to ensure valid results. The results should be analyzed and evaluated and appropriate documented information should be retained as evidence. This output will demonstrate conformity of products and services to requirements and assess many of the areas listed below.

Monitoring can be done through weekly production meetings, inspections, verifications, compliance reviews, calibrations, audits, walkthroughs, etc. This will ensure operational efficiency and effectiveness. Should there be any nonconformances, these will be managed through a corrective action system.

Key Areas That May Be Monitored

1. Customer satisfaction and complaints

2. Business operations (Assess conformity and effectiveness of the management system, that strategic planning has been implemented, assessing the performance of processes and external provider's services)

    a. Financial control

    b. Legislation compliance—quality, environment, health and safety

    c. Objectives, targets, programs, KPI

    d. Continual improvement

    e. Best available technology and industry trends

    f. Supply chain—purchasing, acquisitions, subcontractor control

    g. Process—quality, environmental impacts and health and safety hazards

    h. Change management

    i. Document management—policies, manual, procedures, forms

    j. Operational control—management system control plan

    k. Analysis—data evaluation

    l. Personnel and supplier performance

        • Internal/subcontractor: Identified, competent, trained, performance

3. Process

    a. Quality

    b. Product acceptance criteria

    c. Safe operating requirements

    d. Statistical techniques

    e. Nonconformances

4. Product

    a. Receiving

    b. In-process

    c. Final inspection and test

5. Equipment and plant maintenance

    a. Material handling—calibration

    b. Preventative maintenance

Objectives

Monitoring helps management identify and assess progress, solve any implementation issues, and ensure that objectives are being met. Objectives should be measurable with key performance indicators (KPI). By monitoring the KPIs the organization can evaluate its success toward defined goals.

Ensure that you understand what is important to your organization to attain, and choose the associated performance indicators so that you can identify potential improvements. The balanced scorecard is a very common way to monitor performance. Your KPIs need to be linked to target values so that they can be assessed for meeting specific requirements.

Supply Chain

Many organizations have software programs in place that provide improved insight into spending and efficiency, in order to stay in compliance with Sarbanes Oxley and prevent overspending. However, procurement needs to not only include this information but also continue to look at risk assessment tied to the product and the supplier, as well as seeking and evaluating alternative solutions.

Does monitoring include information related to the supplier's ongoing ability to meet contract requirements and a review of any deviation or nonperformance by the supplier? Do you monitor and have objective evidence related to the supplier's capability, quality assurance program implementation, performance, and necessary follow-up actions? How is this tracked and reported, and to whom? The goods and services may include ongoing management of a contract or the disposal of materials at the end of their life cycle, which also requires monitoring.

Many organizations outsource their supply chain logistics, which can have an impact on customer satisfaction. An organization needs to keep a close focus on quality control of this service regarding confidentiality requirements, conflicts of interest, compliance with legal requirements, delivery performance, customer service, budgeting, and reporting of all procurement requirements to key stakeholders.

Monitoring quality performance of your key suppliers is important regarding global supply of materials and outsourcing of processes. Records of the results of supply chain evaluations and any necessary actions should be kept.

Monitoring–Compliance

The appropriate manager or supervisor will ensure that monitoring and measurement of various parameters are conducted as required to maintain legal compliance in quality, environment, health and safety, and financial areas and report to top management. It is outlined in the revised quality management system for 2015 that top management needs the understanding of legal requirements and issues arising from legal, technological, competitive, cultural, social, economic and natural environment, whether international, national, regional or local that are relevant to its purpose and strategic direction affecting its ability to achieve its management system.

Your organization may have a separate position for handling compliance reviews or audits, such as environmental monitoring done by an environmental engineer/coordinator or auditor. It may do regular, ongoing monitoring of legal requirements tied to environmental areas, such as certificate of approval requirements for stack emissions levels and reporting, hazardous waste disposal volumes and manifesting, and spill response reporting. A third party may be contracted to review legal and other requirements (regulations, corporate, union, codes of practice) every year to ensure ongoing compliance.

Noncompliance is a nonconformance to the management system. It is also a go-to-jail card for managers, coupled with huge fines not only for the organization but also, in some areas, for the managers. It is critical to manage your nonconformances through one system, so that standardization of handling, identifying root causes, and monitoring of all nonconformances is part of the process, ensuring proper management review. Many organizations leave noncompliance issues in reports which can be forgotten about, but a nonconformance-corrective action system will track its root cause, corrective action and verification, until it is closed.

Monitoring and Measurement of Processes

In order to have production/service control, information must be available that describes the characteristics of the product or service and the suitable requirements (equipment for production) for operations, as well as measuring and monitoring equipment. This is where your quality control plan, which has been expanded to a management system control plan, can be used, listing all processes, their risks and control methods.

Ongoing monitoring, tied to your management system control plan, can help you to identify and improve your processes, regarding, for example, the need to increase resources or change to automation or new technology, so that you can streamline and improve performance at your organization.

Process Monitoring Steps

1. Do a process map. This will help you visually see the dynamics of your processes and how they interrelate, as well as the number of steps required to complete each task. Time costs every company. Conduct inspections (quality, environment, health and safety).
2. Review the data that was tied to the monitoring of the process to analyze performance.
3. Identify improvement opportunities based on the evaluation.
4. Make improvement changes in the management system for the new way of doing business.
5. Monitor changes to ensure benefit to the company.

Product/Service

Monitoring and control of suitable parameters and product characteristics ensure products/service meet the specified customer requirements. Conformance with workmanship standards is confirmed through inspection and supplier reports.

Inspection records and test results need to be maintained as objective evidence. Analysis of test or inspection results is used to identify problems. The record of product monitoring needs to include the person viewing the product, confirming the nonconforming product, and also the person authorizing release.

Control of Nonconforming Product or Service

The quality control or QC department is usually responsible for the management of nonconforming product by implementing and maintaining comprehensive methods and reports for monitoring and measuring the characteristics of the product, to verify requirements are being met throughout the product realization processes, in accordance with quality requirements, as outlined on the quality control plan.

Verification of customer specification, legal requirements, product characteristics, equipment, etc. would be addressed at suitable measurement location points. Inspections or tests resulting in unacceptable or nonconforming products would be recorded, segregated, and adequately identified to prevent further use until disposition.

Notification will be given to applicable managers about relevant functions of the nonconforming product(s), and there may be release or acceptance under concessions by relevant authorities where the product could be reworked or repaired, depending on circumstance. When a nonconforming product is corrected, it will be subject to reverification. Records should indicate the authority responsible for submission and release of products and delivery of services to the customer.

Issues tied with products or services from external providers may be monitored and managed through the supply chain, however it is advisable to have one central area for tracking all nonconforming product, which may be in your nonconformance-corrective action system.

Equipment

Monitoring includes the control of monitoring and measuring equipment. Performance cannot be accurate if the machinery has not been calibrated and verified to provide the correct measurements.

Analysis of Information

Through the analysis of information comes the insight for change and the need to take action. It is important to have a process in place to manage your changes to ensure resources are assigned and the management system structure is reviewed regarding how this change will impact all areas. This process can be used for changes such as specifications, processes (machine technique), equipment, raw material, or packaging, or any other change.

Monitoring any changes at the organization related to processes, materials, and equipment through the management of change process ensures the review of risks and controls. A reexamination needs to be done after the change as well.

Evaluation

The quality standard revision, ISO 9001:2015, now emphasizes evaluation. An organization will now look to evaluation, and this brings to the forefront requirements to make the organization data-driven so that the monitoring will include evaluation of the data that is being kept.

Evaluation is focused on lessons learned and bringing them into the decision-making process for continual improvement. Here is where the manager looks at data to drive business decisions; therefore, the data needs to be measurable, having key metrics or performance indicators.

The evaluation needs to be objective so that it provides credible information. Evaluation addresses the analysis of data or, digging deeper, looks at root causes and the bigger picture.

Evaluation looks at your business risks and opportunities for the future and the fulfillment of objectives, where transparency is essential for investors, third-party registrars, corporate head offices, and the public, who are interested in the results of something.

Regardless of what monitoring and evaluation you are doing, it is imperative that the data is relevant, reliable, and complete; otherwise you will be making incorrect decisions.

Senior management of an organization analyzes data from various sources to assess performance against plans, objectives, or criteria. The management system itself has systems in place, such as the internal audit process and a nonconforming product and nonconformance system that assist in the analysis and review of your management system.

Assess & Reflect #47

PERFORMANCE EVALUATION

What does our organization need to monitor and measure? How?

What methods do we use for monitoring performance?

Is our data providing value?

_____

_____

_____

_____

_____

_____

_____

_____

_____

_____

_____

_____

_____

_____

_____

_____

_____

_____

_____

_____

_____

_____

_____

_____

_____

Internal Audit

To ensure ongoing management system structures are in place that will drive and manage your business accomplishments, internal process audits are conducted to ensure effectiveness and efficiency of operations.

Auditors need to be trained in the following: the management system standard requirements (Quality—ISO 9001, Environment—ISO 14001, Occupational Health and Safety—OHSAS 18001), as well as your corporate requirements and Auditing Guidelines—ISO 19011, in order to conduct internal audits on your processes.

Having trained thousands of auditors since 1995, through my own company and working with major registrars, such as British Standards Institute (BSI), QMI SaiGlobal, and Intertek, I would recommend your internal auditors conduct ongoing monthly process audits, of one day's duration, per month on your processes throughout the year. This way your organization stays current on the status of what is happening at your organization and auditors stay competent in conducting audits.

Many organizations do not understand the value of the internal audit process, possibly because the auditors they have chosen do not have enough business management background to audit the management system processes. The reports they have provided in the past to the company do not assist in improving the structure or performance of the company's operations. For this reason, it may be advisable to contract third-party auditors, who have managed business operations and understand management systems, having worked with many organizations. Their varied management system experience insight, as well as audit protocols, would provide an unbiased report, outlining opportunities for improvement. The timeline for external internal audits can be according to your organization's size, processes, and risks, and can be done quarterly, every six months or yearly, depending on the importance of keeping up-to-date verification on your management system.

The audit plan's objectives should be to address that the requirements of the management system meet international standards and corporate requirements. The audit would ensure that customer requirements and opportunities for improvement for customer satisfaction are met. Another example of an objective for your audits is to check the effectiveness of processes, and what opportunities for improvement (OFIs) they would recommend to top management. Here is an opportunity to support innovation.

Process Audits—Three-Step Process

Process audits can also follow Pilot's three steps—Identify, Insure, Improve—as this would provide a standardized approach, providing consistency in how they look at all processes at your organization.

Step One, Identify: The auditor would look at the process to see if managers and employees understand the organization, its risks and legal requirements tied to the process they are working with, and the controls needed. Past nonconformances would be reviewed. He or she would review the objectives that have been set for the process and the status of the project(s) and strategic plans and any input to the success or failure of the plan. The policy statement is reviewed as to what it means to workers in that particular process, in order to get a clear understanding of what the workers see as the key values and principles for the organization.

Step Two, Insure: The auditor reviews the documentation (specifications, control plans, procedures, records, quality control, and responsibilities) requirements for the process, the applicable procedures, and work instructions. Are they being followed—why or why not? There will be a review of infrastructure and working environment of the process. What communication methods are used to improve performance—for example, "OneStep Lessons"? Training and competency will be checked. How are changes dealt with—for example, process changes and improvements? What nonconforming products have been found in the process and why? There will be a review of any outsourced work done on that process, maintenance of equipment, calibration, etc. What customer focus is required in the process? Are customer requirements being met in this process? How? Are there any issues tied to the supply chain—for example, design or production?

Step Three, Improve: What monitoring and measurement is done in this process (inspections-environment, health and safety, quality control, external reviews – insurance reports, compliance audits, nonconformances)? What is its status? How can it be improved? Can any areas be improved through automation and changes? Review of analysis of data related to this process and its evaluation results. What recommendations would managers and workers in this process suggest for improvement to the operation or the organization's management system processes? Has any "innovation" come from this process for improvement? What was it? Was it rewarded? In the management review of the process, what has been discussed, and are there any concerns or action items?

Management Review

Many executives find meetings unproductive and a waste of time with more talk and less action. However, if properly managed, meetings can be effective and have results.

Productive Meetings

Table 14.1 provides a few suggestions to make your meetings more productive.

TABLE 14.1	
Suggestions for a Productive Meeting	
Identify	
Purpose of meeting	Are you: reviewing, discussing, decision making, connecting? Is the meeting necessary?
	What will the inputs and outputs be? Agenda: topics, presenters, action needed (decision, action assignment), supporting material
	Regular staff meetings may have a common template for the meeting.
Time factor	Is timing correct? Schedule. Reduce meeting times in half—30 minutes, maximum one hour. Meet regularly, even 15 to 30 minutes. Sufficient meeting notification. Those more than 15 minutes late can't participate. Start on time and end on time or earlier.
	Meetings can be online, in person, or by phone.

(continued)

(Continued)	
Identify	
Participants	Fewer people. Productivity can go down with increased number of participants. Who can provide needed information, expertise, and support?
Insure	
Preparation	Participants are to prepare for meeting in advance.
	Restate at beginning of meeting: agenda, meeting purpose, and outcomes to be accomplished.
Control	Who called the meeting – you are in charge. Provide leadership in group participation and interaction at meeting, not allowing individuals to dominate. Full participation: "What do you think?" No diversion of attention, with phones, emails, or other discussions. Look at time wasters.
	Appoint someone to take minutes of meeting, outcomes reached with action items, and who will champion them.
	Visual control—whiteboard or flipchart
Improve	
Action items	Summarize action items. Keep focus on purpose with three to five action items. Too many result in inactivity. Determine next meeting time. Minutes sent out within 24 hours.
	Thank participants for attending.

Management reviews to international standards, looks at the continuing suitability, adequacy, and effectiveness of the management system(s) (ISO 9-14-18), as well as changes required and improvements (OFI). The review covers both inputs and outputs, which do not need to be reviewed all at once, and may be done over a period of time. Complete reviews may be done tied to quarterly budgets, as an example. The policy statement should be reviewed at least yearly for an update.

The *inputs* to the management review would include:

- Information from previous management review meetings
- Changes in external and internal issues relevant to management system, including strategic direction
- Information on performance of the management system, results of internal audit(s), communication/customer feedback, and effectiveness of meeting customer satisfaction

- Monitoring and measurement results on process performance, environment/health and safety performance and product conformity/productivity/profits, status of nonconformances and corrective actions, accidents/incidents
- Changes to management system (legal, policy, objectives/KPIs, management system), technology, innovation
- Recommendations for improvement for quality, environment, health and safety, and new opportunities for continual improvement
- Adequacy of resources for maintaining an effective management system
- Effectiveness of actions taken to address risks and opportunities

The *outputs* from the management review will include any decisions and actions related to:

- What actions need to be taken or changes need to be made to continually improve the effectiveness of company's IMS and related processes?
- What new objectives and targets need to be set, and who will manage them? What actions are needed to continually improve products/services, meet customer requirements, and improve customer satisfaction?

Improvement

Top management demonstrates leadership and commitment with an ongoing objective for a management system to continually review opportunities for improvement, through the effective application of the management system and its processes for its sustainability and success. There are many processes that can be used in improvement:

- Customer satisfaction will bring sustainable profitability. Ask clients what you are doing well and how you can improve.
- Continuous improvement—setting of strategic plans or goals, policy, objectives and targets with action plans (projects with budgets or measurables, timelines, senior management accountability, and process ownership) for the sustainability and success

(profitability) of the organization (change management—buy-in).

- Ensuring the integration of management system requirements into the organization's business processes.
- Determining the risks and opportunities that need to be addressed to achieve continual improvement.
- Ensuring resources needed are available (re-organization, mentoring programs), technology, automation.
- Communicating the importance of effective management and conforming to the management system, and ensuring promotion of customer focus throughout the organization.
- Engaging, directing, and supporting persons to contribute to its effectiveness through creativity and innovation.
- Ensuring integrity of the management system is maintained when changes are planned and implemented (improvement through breakthrough).
- Monitoring and measurement, analysis and evaluation, internal audit, management reviews used to determine need of opportunities for improvement within the management system.
- Reporting on performance of the management system on opportunities for improvement and the need for change or innovation.
- Process of handling nonconformity and corrective action.

Nonconformity–Corrective Action

Your organization needs to identify what it classes as a nonconformity. A nonconformity can be not meeting planned requirements.

These requirements could be the corporate requirements, management system, not following procedures/work instructions/planned arrangements, legal/noncompliance issues, accidents or emergency situations, nonconforming products, supplier nonconformances, complaints, etc. When a nonconformity occurs, your organization needs to react to the nonconformity as applicable, to take action to control and correct it and deal with the consequences. Then the nonconformity should be evaluated for the need for corrective action to eliminate the cause of it so that it does not recur or occur elsewhere.

Having all nonconformities and corrective action reports in one database (nonconformity system) is helpful to monitor what is not meeting requirements. These nonconformities can be categorized for ease of review.

It may be the ISO coordinator who manages the records of all nonconformances implemented and closed. The nonconformance report (sometimes referred to as CAR—corrective action report) would be sent to the applicable department manager/supervisor for review and to evaluate the need for corrective action, to determine the cause (root-cause analysis), and implement any action required to eliminate the cause(s). They should also determine if similar nonconformities exits or could potentially occur in their evaluation. The corrective action report is to be completed, in a timely manner to resolve problems and their causes. A review of any changes to the management system would also be required. Verification of the corrective action's effectiveness and necessary changes to the management system could then be completed by the coordinator, auditor, or chosen individual.

An evaluation of nonconformities should be conducted to see if there are any trends or patterns of occurrence.

Management review meetings should continually focus on what nonconformities are applicable to what processes and the status of corrective actions.

Assess & Reflect #48

WHERE DO WE STAND? WHAT ARE WE DOING WELL?
WHAT CAN WE IMPROVE? WHAT CAN WE DO DIFFERENTLY? WHAT
SHOULD WE STOP DOING?
WHAT OPPORTUNITIES FOR IMPROVEMENT WERE OUTLINED IN THE
FOLLOWING:

Customer satisfaction: What did our customers tell us that we are doing well? What do they value? What did they tell us needed improvement?

Objectives: What objectives are we presently working on? (projects, Six Sigma) Are we working on the right things? Are our metrics correct for the process? What buy-in do we have from our stakeholders (employees, contractors, customers)?

Change management: How do we link the changes (innovation) to the past controls (consistency)? How do we ensure leadership and sustainability of the change (project)?

Risk management: What areas tied with risk have we improved in?

Internal and third-party audit findings: What areas do we need to improve on in our management system processes? What areas do we need to improve on in our product/service? What compliance areas (legal) need to be addressed?

Management reviews: What do our management reviews focus on for improvement?

_____

_____

_____

_____

_____

_____

_____

_____

_____

_____

CHAPTER 15

Conclusion

F or the CEO of a company, the following conclusions can be reached, tied with the research that has been outlined in this book. The current competitive landscape results are quoted from the World Economic Forum.

The onus is on the CEO and top management to assess, reflect, and act to ensure the business sustainability of their organization. This book has provided you with questions to ask and get answers for to help in this leadership. The onset of the grey tsunami could be a ripple or a tidal wave, depending on whether you are prepared to deal with the aging population and the upcoming tech-savvy generation. You must be the visionary who brings about management system integration and automation with innovation and technology.

Competitive Landscape

Companies looking for insight into the competitive landscape of some 148 economies can go to www.weforum.org/reports/global -competitiveness-report for the most comprehensive assessment of national competitiveness worldwide. The need for innovation is outlined in the report's preface:

> In the current context, policymakers must avoid complacency and press ahead with the structural reforms and critical investments required to ensure that their countries can provide a prosperous environment and employment for their citizens.

They must identify and strengthen the transformative forces that will drive future economic growth. Particularly important will be the ability of economies to create new value-added products, processes, and business models through innovation.

Going forward, this means that the traditional distinction between countries being "developed" or "developing" will become less relevant and we will instead differentiate among countries based on whether they are "innovation rich" or "innovation poor."

Mr. Klaus Schwab, Executive Chairman, World Economic Forum

As a Leader

I Know That

- Our business world is the global marketplace. Our management system processes need to be understood, integrated, automated, and managed to international standards.
- Social media has transformed the way we do business.
- Transparency disclosure practices are here to stay.
- Customers require a product/service consistency, whether it is in the product itself, packaging requirements, delivery times, etc. Are we in the game?
- The clock is ticking and baby boomers are leaving the workplace; we need succession planning in our organization.
- Process risks need to be identified and managed.
- Changes need to be managed.
- Innovation and technology keep us in the marketplace.

I Am the Visionary

As a manager, director, or leader in the organization, I am the visionary who will make the future for the organization. Choices need to be made and urgency is upon us. Leaders ask questions—questions like the following, which I have answered.

- Where will our business be in the next two to five years?
- What will be our top three business challenges?

- What are our principles, plans for performance, productivity, and profits?

I need to be able to communicate our principles and plans successfully to our stakeholders.

If you can't explain it simply, you don't understand it well enough.

Albert Einstein

I Learned

How you put these three areas in use for the future will determine where we are in the race:

1. Mobility (Internet, mobile devices)
2. The cloud
3. Instant analysis of data (for decision making and real-time data)

Pilot Project—Management System Makeover™ Driving Sustainability to Business Success

As a leader in business, I will need to turn corporate strategy into system thinking by asking questions, being creative, and innovating in order to improve, and being progressive in automation and technology in order to be competitive.

These three steps—Identify, Insure, Improve—are important steps in the success of implementing and auditing an integrated business management system driving our mission.

The Pilot project for a management system makeover will provide the ability to sustain or invest now for the future, empowering our organization to be successful in the global marketplace.

To all my readers:

I wish that this book, *Driving Sustainability to Business Success—The DS Factor*, will be an agent for change to provide you, as a leader, with an opportunity to assess and reflect, and inspire you to act, to drive your business to success in this competitive global marketplace. When we can be successful in our businesses, we can reach out to help sustain others.

Success requires you as a leader to ask questions, to solve problems, to think or imagine beyond boundaries, to take calculated risks and to take action. Remember there is no such word as "can't"; you can do anything you put your mind to, write it down, be open to opportunities. Be innovative, creative, use new technology. Build your mission by understanding your customers and ensuring your integrated management system structure and implementation team are built on solid principles that support improvement and engagement for defined and measurable sustainability for customer satisfaction and business success.

Jayne Pilot
Pilot Performance Resources Management Inc.
www.pilotims.com

About the Author
—M. Jayne Pilot

M. Jayne Pilot has been CEO of Pilot Performance Resources Management Inc. (www.pilotims.com) since 1994, located in Brampton (Greater Toronto Area), Ontario.

She is a demonstrated industry leader as an author, speaker, consultant, auditor, and trainer in business management systems and international standards (ISO), working with major corporations in all business sectors in North America. She is a speaker on "Driving Business Sustainability" with boards of trade and many sponsors, providing CEOs a place to learn, showcase, and meet other high achievers working in the global marketplace.

She is recognized by her peers and industry, receiving many awards of recognition: Canada's Most Powerful Women – Top 100 by WXN; Canadian Professional of the Year – Canada Pakistan Business Council; Business Award (twice)–City of Brampton Economic Development and Trade; Pinnacle Award–Women of Distinction; President's

Award – Browning Ferris Industries-International firsts for Medical Waste, International Waste and Diabetic Depot Systems.

Early in her career, she received several diplomas in business management and arts and science from Confederation College, and a certificate from the School of Management at Banff Centre. She is a certified ISO management system auditor and has maintained ongoing professional development through extensive workshops, seminars, and online education tied to environment, health and safety, quality, and auditing.

She has over 30 years of business management and innovative technology work experience with Fortune 500 companies and governments. She initiated a number of international firsts in sustainability, in the environmental field in waste management, and in the ISO management system field, developing standards, policy, and training for the auditing profession in Canada and United States. She sat on the plenary group for auditor certification in Canada, organized by the Chartered Accountants of Canada, was a Director with the Auditing Association of Canada, and represented Canadian industry on ISO 14001 for NAFTA conference, organized by the Conference Board of Canada in the early 1990s.

Pilot Performance Resources Management Inc.'s goal was to provide management with an understanding of effective and efficient management systems to meet international standards and help sustain their businesses to work in a global marketplace. These programs offer a simple process for implementation through their training and consulting services. Her innovative "Three-Step Process—Identify, Insure, Improve" has been used by thousands of organizations to implement management system structures meeting international standards.

Her guidebook *ISO 9001*, published by Specialty Technical Publishers, came out in 2002 and is updated quarterly to help organizations implement and integrate quality with environment and health and safety, utilizing her Three-Step Process. Her client Zochem was the first in North America to be registered by BSI as meeting an integrated management system. She has many published articles on management systems and environment in industry magazines, including *ISO Management Systems*, *Government Buyer*, *Air & Waste*, and *Hazmat*.

Jayne is involved internationally and sits on the ISO/TC 176 Quality Management Technical Committee as an associate member on quality management and the Mirror Committee on Quality with Standards Council of Canada, participating in international standards development activities. She is the vice president of the Canada-Pakistan Business Council and member of the International Committee with the Brampton Board of Trade, as well as a business ambassador for the City of Brampton. She is a member of the Training Committee for the U.S. Board of Environment, Health & Safety Auditor Certification and past director of the Auditing Association of Canada.

She is active on many environmental committees, including cochair of Algonquin Power Waste to energy community liaison (now Emerald Green) since 1993 and the City of Brampton's Environmental Committee. In the past she was a very active member with the Air and Waste Management Association international committee.

Jayne is an active member of the Rotary Club of Brampton and supports Rotary International's focus in promoting peace, preventing diseases, providing access to clean water and sanitation, enhancing maternal and child health, improving basic education and literacy, and helping communities develop.

Index